TRANCE DANCE

Frank Natale is Founder and President of the Natale Institute for Experiential Education, which runs seminars worldwide on Trance Dancing and drumming, as well as courses in communication, self-esteem and sexuality.

by the same author

Mastering Alive Relationships

Trance Dance

THE DANCE OF LIFE

Frank Natale

ELEMENT
Shaftesbury, Dorset ● Rockport, Massachusetts
Brisbane, Queensland

© Frank Natale 1995

First published in Great Britain in 1995 by
Element Books Limited
Shaftesbury, Dorset SP7 8BP

Published in the USA in 1995 by
Element Books, Inc
PO Box 830, Rockport, MA 01966

Published in Australia in 1995 by
Element Books Limited
for Jacaranda Wiley Limited
33 Park Road, Milton, Brisbane 4064

Cover illustration by Michael Dunning
Text illustrations by Anthea Helliwell
Cover design by Max Fairbrother
Page design by Roger Lightfoot
Typeset by WestKey Limited, Falmouth, Cornwall
Printed and bound in Great Britain by Biddles Ltd, Guildford and
King's Lynn

British Library Cataloguing in Publication
data available

Library of Congress Cataloging in Publication Data

Natale, Frank.
    Trance dance: the dance of life / Frank Natale.
    1. Ecstasy–Miscellanea. 2. Shamanism–Miscellanea.
3. Dancing–Religious aspects–Miscellanea. I. Title.
BL626.N38 1995
291.3–dc20 95-12177

ISBN 1-85230-702-1

 *Acknowledgements*

I acknowledge with deep gratitude: 40,000 years of shamanic Trance Dancing cultures throughout the world; Ayman Sawaf for continued support, generosity and friendship; soul sister Gabrielle Roth, eternal soul brother Veeresh, and Bhagwan Rajneesh (Osho) for their demonstration that music and dance heal. Also Chiara Bosio for the section on making a mask and Maruschi Magyarosy for her contribution to Chapter 9.

Many thanks to *Parabola* and the estate of D M Dooling for permission to reprint an excerpt from D M Dooling's 'Lord of the Dance' which appeared in *Parabola* Magazine.

Special thanks to my early mentors, Lionel Hampton, Tito Puente, Count Basie and Paulie La Playa, for encouraging me to dance professionally at the New York Palladium as 'The Kid' when I was 16. And most of all to my staff, friends and Trance Dance Presenters around the world.

Dedication

This book is dedicated to you, the Dancer, for when you know how to breathe consciously and move from your heart, you will immediately access a state of euphoria, that Trance Dance state our shamanic ancestors called 'ecstasy'.

My intent is to reveal this and other simple truths to all people around the world, so that together we become a species of Trance Dancing Humans.

Dance with Respect, Passion and Love.

Professor Trance and The Energizers
(Frank Natale)

Contents

Introduction

I became consciously interested in shamanism in 1980 but dismissed it at first as pure superstition. I believed it was an ancient curiosity with little power, having no therapeutic or spiritual value.

While teaching the 'Skills for the New Age' seminar series, I was too often out of my body. I began to miss falling in love, hanging out with friends, being touched, laughing and having sex. Old diseases returned to my body; friends were offended by what they perceived to be aloofness. I felt neither pleasure nor pain, only the objective floating so many of my students called 'bliss'.

Then the rebel within my soul began to speak, 'Dance, move that body, heal it . . .'

My rebellious Spirit, whom I have come to know as my passionate Energizer, continued to direct me: 'Follow your passion. Follow the natural path.' I began to become fascinated by earth-grounded spirituality, especially Goddess worship and shamanism. The Goddess, the earth and shamanism suddenly were present everywhere. Through these I discovered timeless cross-cultural spiritual practices, such as drumming, mandala and mask making, Trance Dancing, ritual dance, journeying for Spirit animals, 'listening to the whispers of our ancestors', soul hunting, power objects, chanting and psychoactive teacher plants. Don't worry if you're not familiar with these ideas – I'll talk much more about them in this book.

Eventually Spirit's direction became my passionate choice. The New Age community validated my choice, as everyone was recognizing the wisdom of our shamanic ancestors and the value of those spiritual cultures whose roots reached back 40,000 years or more. These were time-tested paths, which existed long before Mohammed, Jesus, Buddha or even Shiva.

I returned home to my body. Health and ecology became priorities by choice. Out-of-body experiences became passé as I celebrated being wholly in my body, at last. My eyes and skin began to clear and vitality filled every aspect of my being.

Of all the shamanic practices, Trance Dancing became my favourite, and it grew into an obsession. I have always loved percussion, dance and altering my consciousness. Trance Dancing became the open space through which Spirit celebrated its existence within me. Such an experience would not surprise shamans: they have been using Trance Dancing as a healing technique for thousands of years.

Through Trance Dancing we alter our consciousness and enter non-ordinary reality or what I call 'the World of Spirit', that world beyond time and space where everything is possible.

Through ancient breath patterns, movement and rhythms which impact the brain, the Trance Dancer begins to see with their senses rather than their eyes. Other times and other forms reveal themselves, and the Trance Dancer's consciousness is filled with the magical world of Spirit. With time and experience, Trance Dancing causes you to think with your heart, as our ancestors did, not with your brain.

While your body dances, your soul travels and remembers, free of the limits of this life, free of the limitation of time and space. Spirit returns home and is embodied within you, the Trance Dancer. Tremendous energy is awakened, spontaneous healing occurs and you are filled with visions of power animals, Spirit guides and nature.

The desperate need for enlightenment, bliss and out-of-body experiences dies and instead your body is filled with your total existence. You are fully present, you are at last content, no longer needing to escape the reality you have agreed to. You are finally filled with love, energy, respect and passion for being alive. You are finally satisfied being a human being.

The new paradigm everyone has been waiting for will not come from the heavens, as we have been promised, or from aliens from outer space, but from our original deity 'Mother Nature'. Trance Dancing inevitably brings us to love, respect and passion, three of the essentials of spirituality. When Spirit enters us we shamelessly move our bodies with orgasmic passion, for this is our true nature. We then begin to experience ecstatic healing, as we consciously breathe and move from inside our hearts.

If we are really to heal ourselves and our planet, we will have to live in our bodies and on our planet, rather than constantly looking for ways to leave them. The best way I know to live passionately in my body is to Trance Dance, inviting Spirit to return home, to embody me and restore me to spiritual wholeness.

It is time to return home to our bodies and our great Mother Nature by celebrating them through dance, as Trance Dancing Humans.

I sincerely invite you to call home to your body all the Spirit you have naively sent away. I encourage all of us to recognize our separation from and conscious betrayal of our planet whose soul we have collectively stolen.

This book will provide you with extraordinary information and time-tested spiritual practices which will empower you with the respect, love and passion needed to heal yourself, friends, loved ones and our planet.

I celebrate with great expectation and excitement you taking your first step into the 'Dance of Life', for more than you can imagine will be revealed to you.

1 Our Trance Dancing Ancestors

Dance as a way to move into trance dates back over 40,000 years, to before recorded civilization. Trance Dancing is a deep and moving altered state of consciousness filled with feelings, other lives in human and prehuman forms, rhythms, old and new smells, masks, transforming shapes, known and unknown faces and places beyond time.

We can actually be there without being required to think consciously about or imagine the experience. These experiences begin to move us rapidly into the eternal flow of life and we stop being the dancer and become the dance. During these magical times we disappear into the sacred Dance of Life, transcend time and space and are filled with the sense of our infinite existence that our ancestors called 'ecstasy'.

Trance Dancing and Christianity

Trance Dancing has played a significant role in the birth of all religion. Even within early Christianity Trance Dancing was used to restore religious seekers to spiritual wholeness.

> To the universe
> Belongs the dancer – Amen

> Whoever does not dance
> Does not know their immortality – Amen

Jesus Christ

Jesus was speaking about the 'Round Dance of the Cross' which is described by John, one of Jesus's closest disciples, in his writings, called the Acts of John. The Acts of John were condemned as heresy in the fifth century by Pope Leo the Great. He decided that 'they contain a hot bed of perversity and should not only be forbidden but altogether removed and burnt with fire'.

Jesus danced with his disciples, so they would recognize their own mystical Christ consciousness and immortality.

According to John, those who danced the Round Dance of the Cross received two benefits:

1 They came to know their own Christ consciousness or Spirit.
2 They learned to transcend the paradox of human suffering and discover their immortality.

Orthodox Christians condemned Trance Dancing, fearful it would rob Christianity of its uniqueness, because pagan religions such as Goddess worship and shamanism had used Trance Dancing as a spiritual practice for thousands of years before Christianity. Dance was used as a way to transcend the physical into ecstasy. In spite of orthodox Christian views, the mandala patterns on the floors of medieval European churches were created so that dancers could Trance Dance on them and become reflections of the 'greater mystery', or what we now call 'non-ordinary reality'. (For more on mandalas see Chapter 8.) My favourite is the mandala in Chartres cathedral. Some worshippers would dance or fall to their knees, while others would crawl or pass out into deep trance.

Trance Dancing around the World

Dancing as a spiritual practice for entering non-ordinary states of reality can be found in thousands of cultures: in the native Navajo Fire Dance and Grass Dance; in masked Balinese dancing; in the Hindu Lord of the Dance, Shiva, with his many arms and legs; in Tai Chi, the spiritual dance of martial art; and in the whirling dance of the Sufi.

The geographical areas where spiritual Trance Dancing was found most frequently include sub-Saharan Africa, the Mediterranean and eastern Eurasia. Some cultures noted for their spiritual Trance Dancing include the North American Eskimo, the Yoruba of western Africa, the Umbanda of Brazil, the Sioux of North America, the Shamans of Siberia, the Vodun of Haiti, the Shango of Trinidad, the Coastal Salish of Canada, the Santeria of Cuba, the Sami of Scandinavia and Huichol of Mexico.

The Umbanda of Brazil are a good example of spiritual Trance Dancers. Umbanda spiritual Trance Dancing can still be found in Brazil near the cities of Rio de Janeiro and San Paolo. Umbanda combines Roman Catholicism and the religious practices of the Yoruba of Africa. The Umbanda believe that while Trance Dancing you are embodied by Spirit and empowered to heal others.

Our Ancestors

Since before time we have listened to the beat of our heart. We first danced in one spot, then we began to move like the animals we worshipped. Then we leaped into the air, imitating the sun and moon. Later we became musicians, used drums, hand bells and drumsticks. We wore masks to lead us beyond our earth-bound reality and allow us to experience all humanity, all ages and all animals.

We wore masks, beat on drums, danced upon mandalas, channelled the whispers of Spirit, reclaimed our 'soul parts' with quartz 'stones of light', lived out our collective dreams through ritual dance and altered our consciousness with teacher plants. All these time-tested practices created spiritual wholeness.

We are the end result of a long line of choices within the animal kingdom. As human beings we are not accustomed to thinking of ourselves as animals. Our neo-cortex or third brain makes us unique. It gives us certain potentials and abilities that no other animal has. At the same time, however, it has led us to forget that we are part of the incredible kingdom called nature and to separate ourselves by believing we are superior, rather than just another form of life.

There is much about being human that is positive. We have come to believe that we are innately violent and aggressive, but when we look at our evolution honestly and openly, the evidence shows that we once lived in a peaceful and deeply respectful partnership with nature and Spirit.

Our ancestors did not live in one state of consciousness. They would move, at will, in and out of different states. The shamans were the priest-doctors of our ancestors, enabling people to relate to the totality of nature and the universe by exploring dimensions other than physical reality. Psycho-active herbs such as ayahuasca, peyote, marijuana, hashish and mushrooms, were viewed as 'teacher plants'. When taken with clear intent, they caused people to connect with Spirit and 'listen to the whispers' (that is, of their ancestors and higher and future selves). Some people now call this 'channelling'. When I talk about 'listening to the whispers', I'm describing the idea of listening to the messages from Spirit, which counsel us when we are available to their input.

Our ancestors worshipped both the heavenly spiritual world and the magical world of nature, which is where our Spirit and physical forms come from respectively. They also knew that animals were worthy of worship and that through feminine qualities one could produce the rebirth of spiritual life, or what we now call 'enlightenment'. Throughout the world teacher plants were used to civilize and to promote the qualities of passion, respect, love, preservation, nurturing and sensitivity, in both men and women.

Descendants of these people still exist, such as the Sami people in northern Scandinavia, the Indians of North, Central and South America, and the aboriginals in Australia and Africa. There are certain spiritual practices that they all do and have been doing for thousands of years, not out of faith or belief but because of trial, error and experience.

Obviously the various cultures have different and unique spiritual practices, but there are some practices that are common to all. One of these is going into trance using drumming. We now know through scientific research that rhythms of 120 or more beats per minute impact the brain in such a way that they alter consciousness.

Our ancestors also ran and danced in combination with special breathing patterns. They ran as fast as they could until they became exhausted. They then would fall down or walk slowly until they felt their energy coming back, and they would run again.

They used passionate sex, for it is comprised of breathing and physical movement which alter consciousness. Your breathing changes during passionate sex and you go into an altered state of consciousness where you are no longer aware of your body. You and your partner hope to lead each other to that trance state of consciousness called 'orgasm'. You go into a deep void; your physical body, ego and consciousness as we know them disappear, even if it is just for a few seconds.

But the most popular way our ancestors went into trance was by Trance Dancing. Dancing for the purpose of altering consciousness dates back 35,000 years or more, in different forms. It persisted in Western culture until about 600 years ago by which time we had eliminated most rituals from our lives.

This lack of ritual in our culture has cost us a great deal, but where we see the greatest damage is in the psyches of our youth. Most of our young people today have no idea what stage of development they are passing through. We have removed all the rites of passage and traditions from our culture in the name of being modern and contemporary. Consequently, young people don't really have any sense of where they are or where they are going. They have become disenchanted, absented from Spirit and magic, incapable of being 'turned on' to life and being human beings.

Suppression, Persecution and Survival

So, dance as a way to evoke Spirit is not a new idea. Unfortunately, its suppression is not new either. Trance Dancing has been perceived as illness and madness, something to be prevented and defended against. This was especially true of the 'possession dancers' of the medieval period.

The following words describe the 'Dance of the Rhine Valley' in the 14th century:

> Amidst our people here is the madness of dance. In every town there now are some who fall into a trance. It drives them night and day. They scarcely stop for breath.

Some of the ways in which Trance Dancing was repressed during the medieval period are quite frightening. The following are just a few:

- In 1507, 30 women were burned alive in Catalonia, Spain.
- In 1580, 900 sorcerers and sorceresses were burned alive in Lorraine, France.
- In 1630, the entire Benedictine convent in Madrid, Spain, was closed.

The beliefs that surrounded these dancers determined how the dancers were treated, rather than any real evidence. For example, the sorcerers of Lorraine were burned by fire for being possessed by Spirits, whereas in Italy the Tarantella dance was encouraged since it resulted from, and was the only cure for, the bite of the tarantula spider. Trance Dancing was viewed as a form of insanity, except when it was an expression of the religious beliefs in power at the time.

But Trance Dance was not wiped out. Its roots are too deep: its origins may be older than humanity, being found in the mating habits of many species – although among primates we find it only in the apes.

Dance itself is rooted in our hearts and our immortal being. In the ecstasy of dance we bridge that separation between this and the other world – that world filled with Goddesses, Gods, Spirits and entities which we have no names or pictures for.

Trance Dancing is a sacred rite, which at times embodies prophetic vision. It manifests the forces of nature, heals the sick and links the dead to their descendants. It assures us of our immortality, therefore providing us with direction and self-esteem. In ancient times it blessed the tribe or clan and returned it to spiritual wholeness.

It is time for us to dance once again.

2 The Energizers

The Ancient Origins

The Energizers were the spiritual visionaries who through direct contact with Spirit achieved ecstatic spiritual wholeness.

The Energizers were the inner circle within the spiritual movement of the Goddess, which occurred before what we now know as civilization, during that period which started 40,000 years ago and continued through the civilizations of ancient Egypt and the Minoans. These cultures were the last to keep the religion of the Goddess before 'the male-dominated single prophet model' took over some 3,000 years ago.

The Gnostics were the Energizers within Christianity, they were the 'knowers', the ones closest to Jesus Christ, until the Popes of AD 100 to 400 persecuted them because they wanted to stop them from Trance Dancing and continuing other spiritual practices rooted in Paganism. The Popes believed that by destroying the Gnostics Christianity would appear to be unique and not show its roots in Pagan Goddess worship.

The Energizers were both men and women. They lived in a time when sex and passion were thought of as legitimate spiritual paths. They awakened the passion within people.

They were shamans who, through entertainment, storytelling, pleasure, sexual seduction, divine wisdom and satisfaction awoke the energy and aliveness within people, causing them to have unique and authentic experiences of ecstasy. They were androgynous, seductive, creative and musical. They were dancers for the most part and many were also musicians and other types of artists.

An Energizer with whom people in the contemporary West will be familiar is Mary Magdalene. Throughout the Christian Bible she is referred to as a friend of Jesus and he spent a great deal of time with her. It is unfortunate that people of her way of life are currently thought of as being immoral. Even in Jesus's time people still worshipped the feminine qualities of nurturing, creativity, sensitivity and sensuality. Magdalene was one of Jesus's teachers; she was the only person to recognize him once he had risen from the dead. The symbol of death and resurrection is the process of Jesus, the man, transforming to Christ consciousness, and Mary, being an Energizer, recognized this.

The nature of Mary Magdalene comes to us in two ways; through the gospels, where she is portrayed as adulterous, and in the earlier scriptures of the Gnostics, where she appears as a true Energizer capable of transforming the mundane with the ecstasy of passion. Both versions show Magdalene as someone who uses the powers of sexual passion as well as being a source of divine wisdom.

Ancient Energizers would have sexual contact with many to arouse their passion and, therefore, their spirituality. Energizers get life moving. Their energy was expressed through the rhythm of the dance, which is why one of their symbols was the power of the drum.

Other examples of Energizers exist in Tibetan Buddhism. The Dakinis were Energizers. Dakini means 'sky-going woman' or 'sky dancer'. Energizers are ecstatic types who live life through sexual passion, dance, music, art and archaic wisdom.

During the shamanic years of the Goddess men and women

served in temples as Energizers. In India they were called 'Devadassi'. They served in the ancient temples as dancers and sexual partners. Some Devadassi exist today in Orissa.

One of the great Energizers of all time was Shiva, Lord of the Dance. I share one of the many legends of the Dance of Shiva, retold by D M Dooling in his 'Lord of the Dance'.

Once long ago, in a certain forest in India, there were ten thousand wicked rishis who taught the people a false teaching. When this came to the ears of the God Shiva, he disguised himself as a wandering yogi and called upon his other-self, Vishnu, to go with him in the form of a beautiful woman to the forest where the rishis lived with their wives. When they arrived, these women were immediately enraptured with the yogi, and the rishis with his lovely wife, so that the whole community was thrown into confusion.

When the rishis saw what was happening, they began to doubt their own eyes and to feel that they were the victims of an illusion. They met together and decided that the newcomers were working an evil spell on them, and in their turn they cast a powerful curse on the yogi and his wife. But it had no effect at all. Gathering their forces, they made a magical fire and evoked from it a ferocious tiger which sprang upon the disguised Shiva. But Shiva lifted the tiger with one hand and, with the little finger of the other, he tore off its skin and flung it around his shoulders for a cloak. Horrified, the rishis fell back and with another incantation they brought forth a huge serpent, which writhed toward Shiva with gaping jaws. Again Shiva lifted it with one hand and coiled it easily around his neck like a garland. Next the rishis produced a fierce goblin, black in colour and armed with a club, who rushed upon the God, only to be pressed under his feet.

And then Shiva, with his foot still on the squirming creature, began to dance. No longer the wandering yogi, he showed himself now as the shining God, his many arms and legs flashing in speed and splendour like the rays of the whirling sun. The rishis were overwhelmed with wonder and fell on their knees before his vision, behind which the heavens opened and the Gods themselves came to watch the glorious dance.

Then through the veil of appearances came Parvati, Shiva's

divine spouse, riding on a white bull and Shiva mounted with her and they rode away to the northern Paradise. The Gods disappeared; the rishis crept away, devotees now of Shiva. Vishnu and his servant Ati-Sheshan, the great snake with a thousand jewelled heads, were left behind in the silence.

When he could move and speak after this dazzling sight, Ati-Sheshan begged Vishnu, 'Lord, let me go in search of Shiva, that I might again behold the wonders of his dance.' And Vishnu gave him permission to follow the divine pair on the white bull.

So Ati-Sheshan came to the northern Paradise and took up the life of an ascetic as a follower of Shiva. After much time had passed, Shiva came to him, riding on a swan, in the likeness of his third self which is Brahma, to put him to the test.

'You have earned the joys of heaven by your austerities,' he told him. 'Ask for what you will.' But Ati-Sheshan replied, 'I do not wish for heaven nor for anything other than to see again the dance of the Shiva.' 'Then you will remain as you are,' said Brahma-Shiva. But the serpent was unmoved; and seeing his sincerity, Shiva assumed his own form and, gently touching his jewelled heads, he began to teach him the true teaching.

'The Universe is of seeming forms,' he said, 'is made of appearances, as the pot is made of clay. The instrument by which it is formed, as the pot by the stick and wheel, is Parvati, my wife; while its first cause, the potter himself, am I. My dance, which you so long to see, is the source of all movement and all action, in its five aspects of creation, preservation, destruction, embodiment and release. The place of the dance, whether it seems to be a sacred shrine or the unclean burning-ground of corpses, is in reality the human heart. Leave now your serpent-form and be born again as a man. Follow my teaching and you will find my shrine where you will see the dance again and all its secrets will be known to you, for it will take place within.'

(Reprinted from *Parabola*, The Magazine of Myth and Tradition, Vol IV, No 2, Summer)

Queen Maeve of Connacht was also one of the great Energizers. She not only promoted battle, but also slept with many men for her own pleasure. Her name in ancient Irish means 'intoxication'. This intoxicating power of the Energizer is also seen in the Peyote women of the North American Indian tribes. They used peyote cactus to alter their consciousness and attain ecstatic trance states of healing and connection to Spirit. Today there is still an established 'Peyote Energizer' within some North American Indian tribes. The non-addictive peyote is taken as a sacrament. Effects of taking peyote include increased colour vision, Spirit communication and sensual arousal. All these aspects are energizing. Energizers see all sensory experience as a path to higher consciousness and use 'teacher plants' to achieve this.

Teacher Plants

We need to talk a bit more about teacher plants at this point, as it's a sensitive issue that often evokes fear in people because of the lack of expert information in our culture.

Teacher plants are an essential part of shamanism, the ancient way of exploring dimensions other than physical reality. They have always been used throughout the world, within the context of a spiritual ritual. We *always* recommend that people *first* experience altered states of consciousness without teacher plants, and only then suggest they also have the experience with teacher plants. This is not to compare; they are two very different experiences. The use of psychoactive plants expedites and enhances the ability of the dancer to achieve a deeper healing state of ecstasy. The plants allow the dancer's visual cortex to open and induce greater clarity of thought and more vivid images in the mind's eye.

As contemporary shamans our responsibility to humanity and especially to our youth is *not* to deny the presence and value of plants within spiritual ritual, but to educate and guide people until they have experienced the value of their use and no longer are at the mercy of ignorant propaganda.

When our shamanic ancestors used plants, the purpose of being 'stoned' or being 'out of it' was non-existent and in fact they believed that plants enlightened and enhanced consciousness and speeded its evolution. They were dispensed during rituals to alter consciousness and to heal. This was done by the tribal elders. Psychoactive substances were not dispensed by drug pushers. The person who provided the 'Flesh of the Gods' was a high elder in the clan or the shaman and therefore they were taken with a reverent consciousness. They were used with the precise intent of expanding, understanding and enriching life experiences.

I have been taking various teacher plants since I was 16. Once I realized that we as a society had neglected our responsibilities as elders of the tribe of humanity, I no longer had any desire to use artificial chemicals or drugs and now only take natural gifts from Spirit and Mother Nature. The desire to use these gifts solely for the purpose of recreation has also almost become non-existent in my life. I have found instead that their use within the context of ritual, whether that be a pipe ceremony with 20 to 40 dancers or an intimate sexual healing with my partner, provides incredible insights and understanding of self, relationships and life.

When psychoactive plants manifest organically through nature they contain within them Spirit and draw us to our real nature and therefore heal us.

When allowed legally, I sometimes provide teacher plants such as psilocybin, ayahuasca, or marijuana to Trance Dance Presenter trainees so they may have an authentic experience of Trance Dancing as their elders did before we denied the power and appreciation of these healing and mind-expanding plants.

All have reported their experience as enlightening and those who regularly use these same substances recreationally were amazed at how powerful their experience was when taken within the context of the ritual purpose and intent. To believe that psychoactive plants are dangerous and harmful is to ignore and deny the planetary wisdom of our ancestors and nature.

As humans we are biochemically very similar to plants and humans and plants have a symbiotic relationship. We cannot survive without them. We literally breathe them to sustain our life and consciousness. They are the *source* of our aliveness and intelligence. This demands that we become more intimate with these gifts of God and Goddess Earth.

We believe that the denial and rejection of these plants is one of the main reasons our species has become so removed from the Great Mother's intelligence with the resulting disease, ecological abuse, crime and so on.

Many of the plants we use, such as yohimbe, ma huang, san pedro, are legal. After 120 years of research and tests Western culture is realizing that alcohol and tobacco are far more dangerous than marijuana, which is why we are seeing more liberal laws throughout Europe. However, many of these plants are classed as illegal substances and you should be aware of the law in your own country before deciding whether to use teacher plants.

Awakening Passion

As we have said, the ancient Energizers made use of plants to awaken the power of the Energizer within themselves and others. They also worshipped the ecstatic act of sharing passion. Energizers invited sexual union. Another one of the great Energizers was Radha. She was often depicted as being in the superior sexual position while she and Krishna were awakening each others' passion. Symbols of Energizers were often incorporated in medieval churches, placed over the door where the faithful passed in and out, so that no one might be so pious as to ignore their passion and desire.

The most common way to awaken passion and desire was through Trance Dancing. In Nigeria, Energizers were often thought of as being as powerful as a king and were allowed to dance without asking permission.

The Goddess Kali from the Hindu mythology is another good example of an Energizer. She is often depicted sitting naked atop a priest and a Hindu monk receiving ecstatic oral sex from these enforcers of religious dogma.

The enforcing of sexually repressive religious dogma and the denial of the passionate Energizer within our society has had a terrible effect upon our life today. The Energizer's powers have been feared since their use in ancient times. The Energizer's emphasis was on dance, wisdom, energy, passion and sex and most of the organized Western religions have removed the presence of the Energizers, referring to them as shameful and immoral. Gnostic scriptures, however, describe the Energizers in a way that causes us to rethink what we have been told. Some of them do not cast an evil picture. For example, they do not describe Eve as a shamed woman who was exiled from paradise, but as a transcending figure who gives life to Adam by offering him fruit from the tree of knowledge – the wisdom of nature, the Great Mother, the intelligence in nature.

Later, the male-dominated religious model changed the three pillars of spirituality. They changed respect and wisdom to love, passion to compassion and dance to bliss. The results are blissful, loving, compassionate people who have lost touch with their original nature, their sexuality, their passion, their creativity, their joy in dancing and making music, their respect and power, their willingness to explore their spirituality through their bodies and through sharing their passion with others.

The Energizers were excessive. They believed that excess

moved them beyond their limits to new freedoms. This is the main reason why the Energizers were eventually persecuted and eliminated from Christian scriptures.

In the days of Goddess worship, the initiates who became Energizers underwent a sexual rite of passage which had to be experienced with a male or female power holder. These Energizers gave the power of female sexuality to both men and women. They would then be empowered to initiate others. During the early Goddess times the power holder was always a woman, and it was only later that the male was also introduced as the initiator of the power.

As Energizers we challenge our conditioned values to find our Energizer within, our rebel within our souls. The Energizer is the denied and ignored rebel within all our souls. All people who are attracted to Trance Dancing are dormant Energizers, life energy forms which have been conditioned to be repressed. The belief system of the Energizers and that of the entire Goddess movement was wisdom, passion and dance. It is these three values that best express the spiritual curriculum of The Natale Institute (TNI – see Appendix 2) and Trance Dancing.

Be sure that the Energizer within you has been awakened and accepted. This is our passion which is normally repressed, shut down, denied and unfortunately only experienced by many as sexuality rather than as a passion or lust for life. We have awakened our Energizer when we feel deep desire and move ourselves towards the satisfaction of that need. When we are willing to have wisdom, healing, sexual fulfilment and anything else that appeases our spiritual hunger. Only then will we know the ecstasy of having awakened and returned to its rightful position the Energizer within all of us. You will know it has been awakened when you begin to experience deep places of delight and satisfaction, when you have used parts of your body and your mind that you have allowed to go unused for long periods of time.

:tual energy flow occurs, the same one referred to in mysticism as 'Kundalini energy', except that through Trance Dancing we awaken this flow of energy almost immediately, rather than through the years of discipline and spiritual practice required by the Eastern model. Because of the power of this energy, we also teach our students to *respect* it – it is the force of both creation and destruction.

Through Trance Dancing, we are bringing about the rebirth of the Energizers, for they have been absent from our society too long, awakening and uniting all the Energizers that lie dormant within the souls of the overly-conditioned humans of this planet. As the next millennium progresses, we will begin to see the feminine energy becoming an increasing power. Our hearts will begin to direct the human race into different ways of perceiving and understanding. We will bring the male energy into balance with the feminine forces of creativity, passion, peace and partnership.

With the return of the Energizers, life will again embrace the female power holder. Revelations about the feminine or heart energy are already being strongly felt in our contemporary world. As I see it, we will at some point be facing non-science, the death of traditional medicine as we know it, and the acceptance of life as boundless. We will accept that the observer actually creates the observed and bring science effectively to a dead end. We will explore the possibilities of extra-sensory perception (ESP) and silent communication. Most importantly, the sexual and sensual attributes of the feminine will become so powerful that a new sense of heightened sensitivity will arise, creating something still more extraordinary, a new sensitivity towards sexuality.

Life in the male brain has given birth to pornography, violence, dissatisfaction and venereal disease. The new Energizers will bring about life in the 'Age of the Heart', which will bring us back to a stronger, softer approach to sex, with a deeper and more sensual approach to relationships.

The New Energizers:
Professor Trance and the Energizers

Professor Trance, also known as Frank Natale, the spiritual elder of the Energizers, has created a neo-shamanic way of life based on the beliefs and practices of ancient shamanism and Goddess worship. All the spiritual practices used meet two criteria. First, they exist in every shamanic culture worldwide, and second, they have been used on our planet for 35,000 to 40,000 years. This means they are so powerful they have transcended nationality and culture and have undergone thousands of years of trial, error and correction and are therefore more scientific than any existing science.

We employ spiritual practices which have been used effectively since before recorded time, since before our modern methods of psychology which are only 70 years old or the male-dominated religious models of Christianity (2,000 years old), Buddhism (2,500 years old), or even Krishna's teaching (5,000 years old). These spiritual practices have been used effectively for 35,000 to 40,000 years.

'Effectively' for me means they create the opportunity for direct spiritual experience rather than the dogmatic interpretations of someone else's spiritual experience by the hierarchy of an organized religion. This is the difference between shamanism and religion. Shamanism believes everyone is a prophet capable of direct contact with Spirit, while organized religion goes on interpreting for us the spiritual experiences of their religious masters. For example, current Christianity goes on teaching its interpretation of what Jesus Christ experienced 2,000 years ago.

Jesus Christ was an Energizer not a Christian, Buddha was an Energizer not a Buddhist. Both were rebels, creators, the rebirthers of spirituality. Energizers are the originators and founders of all religions.

Energizers reincarnate whenever collective religion

becomes dogmatic and obsessed with fear. We return to reawaken spirituality through our passionate way of life.

Beliefs and Practices of the New Energizers

As new Energizers we create the opportunity for self-realization through the rites of passage presented to us in daily life. Each Energizer has their own individual relationship to Spirit.

The neo-shamanic cross-cultural practices of the new Energizers are: Trance Dancing, soul hunting, mask and ceremonial costume making, the use of power objects, energy work, drumming, the awakening of passion in ourselves and others through sexual seduction, the use of teacher plants within a spiritual ceremony or ritual, initiation rituals such as the touch of passion, and conscious breathing to alter our consciousness.

I've already talked about many of these practices but some may still be unfamiliar. Soul hunting, for example, is connected with the idea of soul loss. This happens when parts of our soul, or Spirit aliveness, are lost during the traumas of life. Soul hunting or soul retrieval heals these traumas and returns the lost soul parts to their body of origin.

Power objects may also need explaining. These can range from aspects of nature, such as trees, animals or crystals, to amulets, drums, clothing, rings, photographs and so on. Power in shamanism means *medicine*, something to heal and support; it's the ability to act. It has nothing to do with the Western concept of power which is about domination and competition. Examples of power objects are:

- *The eagle.* Because it flies so high towards the sun, it has male energy and power, the power of the overview, the big picture.

- *The bear*. Because it hibernates it has the power of contemplation, meditation, inner vision.
- *Quartz crystals*. These contain the intelligence of our ancestors. They are also called 'stones of light'. I hold one in my hand when answering questions.

The symbols of the new Energizers are the drum, the pipe and the serpent. The rhythm of the drum symbolizes the synchronicity of the rhythms of our Great Mother Earth and all the living forms she has given birth to, including human, animal, plant and mineral life forms. These rhythms are in synchronicity with the rhythms of the sun, the moon and the stars. The pipe represents our ability to expand our consciousness and communicate with a universe of active intelligence through the use of teacher plants, to touch Logos, a creature of pure intelligence, and to experience the wholeness of ecstasy. The serpent symbolizes the feminine yet androgynous wave movements of energy which heal the body, awaken our passion and enlighten our consciousness.

As Energizers we are the living link between our future as humans and what is primal, primitive and incomprehensibly ancient within us.

As Energizers we recognize the feminine values and qualities as the only legitimate path at present to greater awareness. We know that these qualities are present in both male and female and that current men and woman are the victims of a male-dominated spiritual model which actually 'blocks' direct spiritual experience.

New Energizers respect and encourage all other forms of spirituality and support their practice unless they inhibit or block the choices of others.

As Energizers we know that conscious breathing, Trance Dancing, drumming, sharing passion, soul hunting, teacher plants and other shamanic spiritual practices are the catalytic motivators for expanding awareness and higher consciousness.

As new Energizers, we know that 'listening to the whispers', the voices we hear in nature, are our future selves calling to us to come forward to fulfil our potential. They are ourselves who exist now in another dimension beyond time/space. They are our future selves.

As Energizers we seduce and initiate others into direct spiritual experience through a variety of legitimate paths. These include the path of passion and sex and as Energizers we respect and protect our own and our partner's body in all appropriate ways. We also follow many other routes to find and give spiritual experience – dance, music, sensuality, respect and knowledge.

As Energizers we recognize romantic love as a modern myth, a concept created by the 12th century troubadours, an illusion which allows individuals to avoid transformation and deny their passion.

We value the use of natural teacher plants for the purpose of dissolving ego and its tight cognitive structure. We also use these regularly to slow time in order to create greater awareness and to keep in balance and civilize the male energy.

We use natural psychoactive substances in our exploration of consciousness and spiritual transformation, and we believe the human species will not advance to new dimensions of evolved consciousness without these nature-given plants; we believe that we are not fully using our human potential nor are we in touch with 'the potential human' unless we have had a series of teacher plant experiences.

New Energizers experience nature and its plants as an older and more highly evolved consciousness. Through the use of teacher plants an animate, actual voice speaks in our heads, addressing important issues from a more integrated and evolved consciousness which normally goes unseen in our daily experience of life.

We understand that authentic spiritual experiences cause

us to question 'the nature of reality' and therefore frighten us. We encourage these experiences and eventually transform fear into excitement.

We view not only humans but also animals, plants and minerals as containing consciousness and therefore being alive. We respect, honour and worship these other life forms and consider them equal to our own.

We recognize the earth as the Great Mother, the original deity, the intelligence in nature, and are clear about humanity's responsibility to co-create through participation with nature.

We respect and feel gratitude for other life forms, recognizing them as living ancestors and an older and wiser consciousness which gave energy and form to humanity. Anything that is natural on earth is alive and conscious.

We as the youngest species of living earth communicate with and learn from the Spirits of nature, recognizing them as the primary source of our wisdom, power and wholeness.

As new Energizers we view 'nature Spirits' as our teachers and friends.

Energizers know that we humans have a symbiotic relationship with plants: we breathe them and they breathe us. Our survival is dependent on their existence. We work toward correcting ecological destruction so as to preserve the human race. We know that the Great Mother existed long before humans and that she will continue to exist even if humans destroy themselves by destroying the plant kingdom.

We have broken away from the isolated view of humanity and acknowledge all living creatures, animals, plants and minerals as our relatives and teachers.

We understand that the Great Mother Earth is alive and conscious. We honour her as the giver and sustainer of life. We experience her as a sacred place and base our lives upon this understanding.

We are both male and female, androgynous in behaviour and temperament; our sexuality is experienced as passionate energy. We enjoy a stronger, yet softer approach to sex, with a deeply sensual, yet freer approach to our intimate relationships.

We choose to think with our hearts as our shamanic ancestors did for 40,000 years rather than with our brains, which is a recent male-led phenomenon.

As Energizers we live in peace, continuously dissolving the seeds of domination and competition in favour of co-operation and partnership.

We reject therapy absent of spiritual presence as being ineffective, causing people to overly analyse themselves and resulting in disempowerment and low self-esteem.

We know that peace and partnership is not possible in a scientific non-spiritual society and that we must shift from a week-end religiousness to a spiritual way of living.

Our emphasis is on living life, rather than on the search for its meaning. Through this living of life we are rewarded with confidence and pleasure, pleasure being the ultimate reward for living life fully now, rather than something one works toward and has to suffer for.

We actively work toward the end of male-dominated history and the rebirth of shamanism, Goddess worship and other earth-grounded spirituality.

We accept that judgements are essential to our survival on the physical plane and that being non-judgemental and loving unconditionally here and now are only a rehearsal for our transformation to the metaphysical. Knowing this prevents us from experiencing the low self-esteem usually associated with therapy and organized religious dogma, which causes us constantly to question and blame ourselves and others.

As Energizers we perceive the symbols of nature and humanity in their original meaning rather than with the distorted significance assigned to them by organized religion. We respect the harmony of the rainbow, the inner concentration of the bear, the femininity of the pyramid, the male/female partnership of the six-pointed star, the wave movement of the serpent which heals, impassions and enlightens, and all the other great symbols for their archaic wisdom.

We laugh, dance, share pleasure and enjoy life without asking permission to do so from anyone.

As Energizers we accept being human as a sufficient and noble purpose, knowing that this humanness is at the dawn of its evolution and that humanity's full potential is incomprehensible at this time.

As Energizers we know that feminism is a legitimate reaction to thousands of years of male domination. Yet it is still a reaction and therefore just another form of domination and not in harmony with the Great Mother who gave birth to sons, daughters and all living creatures.

New Energizers know that creating is to humans what flight is to birds and swimming is to fish. If we must assign a purpose to our species it would be our ability to co-create with the Great Mother. We understand that our unique ability to create is what will disappear if humanity's greatest disease, the victim mentality, gains control.

Energizers recognize magic as the opposite of logic and therefore acknowledge and welcome its existence in our daily life. We trust magic and create ways for it to manifest in our life. We also know that our need to understand everything – a masculine quality – is what kills magic.

Energizers know that magic and power unfold gradually. We do not try to rush or push them. The nature Spirits recognize our individual potential and abilities and, in their time, decide which powers to share with us. The Great Mother herself empowers and chooses us when we are ready to co-create with her.

Initiation

To become an Energizer requires seven or more 'energized experiences' in the company of a 'realized' energy power holder. These energized experiences occur physically, emotionally and mentally, combined always with spiritual experience which transforms the nature of the initiate's reality. These energized experiences normally occur through Trance Dance, soul hunting, teacher plants and other neo-shamanic spiritual practices.

The completion of the initiation is determined by the initiates themselves any time after seven 'energized experiences', at which time the initiate is interviewed by a power-holding Energizer. After the interview the initiate is confirmed by divination and given the Touch of Passion initiation ritual. Once energized, people experience passionate waves of energy so regularly that they perceive them as a way of being rather than isolated experiences.

3 The Healing Power of Trance Dance

The Power of Movement

Through the movement of Trance Dancing you invite the power of Spirit to reside within you. Experiences of this life, lives past, even those in pre-human form, are re-created by the presence of Spirit. Once you allow Spirit to dance within, you will be fully present. This is the path to healing and wholeness.

Far too often we are outside our bodies. To be conscious and enlightened, Spirit must fill our bodies. Trance Dancing is an invitation to Spirit to embody us. When Spirit accepts, we dance from the inside out. We see and experience ourselves through the eternal senses of Spirit, absent of our conditioning and the limits of ordinary reality.

First you must awaken the Energizer within, feel the power of your breath moving in and out, let go of your 'head' and limiting cognitive structure. Then without resistance you will find yourself in trance.

Anyone can Trance Dance because there are no steps. Spirit knows the steps and once awakened and embodied, the Spirit within will take over. There is great joy in rediscovering our Spirit dancing. This dancing is unique to each of us because our body moves in ways beyond our normal reality. Whether these movements are smooth or chaotic, they are always related in some way to our ancient experiences in the evolution of our consciousness. Many of these experiences are joyful discoveries of lives past and others have pain and trauma as their predominant emotion. Trance Dancing empowers you to relive and gain understanding of traumatic events, and to release painful memories so that they no longer interfere in this life.

It is important to remember that there is no right way to Trance Dance. It's your dance, unique to you, and not an external presentation. Trance Dancing has nothing to do with the expectations of others and all to do with revealing the mystery of our timeless existence. Trance Dancing is relaxing, energizing and, most importantly, healing – which is the intent of all shamanic spiritual practice. Through Trance Dance, we awaken the body's natural movement. We reconnect with Spirit and our native animal energy. This is the start of us being fully present in our bodies, empowering us to re-experience the evolution of our consciousness.

Everyone has their own rhythm and movement and with experience you discover the rhythm and music that move you.

Trance Dancing is great natural exercise, an easy and vibrant form of moving trance, and one of the most complete methods of healing known, for it heals body, mind and emotions, by inviting Spirit into this life and revealing other lives, known and unknown.

When you see someone else Trance Dancing it is easy to see its healing power in the freedom of expression, the Spirit that radiates in the dancer's face. In Trance Dance you have permission to be totally yourself so that you can pour your being into that space which connects you deeply with everyone and everything.

Dancing is one of the greatest pleasures of life, a true gift when we do it naturally, without controlling and guiding our movement. When we dance beyond any expected form or style, we can explore and release our natural flow of thoughts and feelings and spontaneously create a healing space.

When we dance spontaneously new movements emerge, opening us to our far memory of times when we have danced before and allowing us to heal traumas and lifelong patterns of disease. When we move into trance and no longer are concerned with what people will think, we free our insecurities and our brain goes clear with relief.

Trance Dancing is for everyone, young and old, male and female, from yuppie stockbrokers to barefoot hippies. All shed their inhibitions when given some simple instruction on how to breathe and how to release movement through dance.

The Reunion with Spirit

Spirit visits the dancer by the dancer's invitation. When this occurs, the dancer disappears and becomes the dance. This can be primitive, aggressive, magical and sometimes sexual.

When Spirit enters each dancer, a collective energy is created which moves everyone beyond their limits until they abandon their conditioned concept of themselves. Their bodies warm and vibrate. Feelings of loneliness and isolation disappear as the music dissolves their separateness and they feel a primal connection not realized in daily life.

Disease and disenchantment are the results of being dis-Spirited. Parts of our Spirit have wandered away for many reasons, leaving us unprotected and vulnerable to disease and struggle. Our illness can be healed by calling Spirit home to our bodies.

Trance Dancing invites Spirit to return home, for all healing must start with a reunion with Spirit and an elimination of the distance which has occurred between human and being.

Once spiritually reunited, Spirit becomes the dancer, dissolving and releasing negative thoughts, creating space for far memory to reveal images and experiences of immortality.

Thoughts are transformed and negative emotions are broken down by our breath and movement. We release sounds of joy, pain, sorrow, anger and passion. Then the body spontaneously in movement releases fatigue and pain until all emotion is cleansed and is experienced as one emotion, that of passion. Passion is the creative force of the universe, our Source, our Spirit in action.

As humans we are 'running mammals' and unless we move our bodies regularly to an optimal cardiovascular heart rate, we will begin to experience low self-esteem and the aches and pains of underachievement.

By Trance Dancing we rediscover our spiritual wholeness and our consciousness moves into spontaneous healing. Consciousness heals spiritually, mentally, emotionally and physically.

Trance Dancing will cause you to be true to your inner movement. It will leave you healed and satisfied, so dance your tears and joy and allow your breath and heartbeats to connect us all until we become a species of Trance Dancing Humans.

Spirit manifests physically as breath and when breath goes in, it moves into the lungs and feeds the blood with the energy that it needs to move through the body. We then experience physical and emotional healing. Breath breaks down the blocks that exist in the emotional body and creates the opportunity for us to feel those emotions and release them. This, obviously coupled with dance, causes you to release them in dramatic and playful ways. Even when you are angry, it is not destructive, for no one is going to be harmed if you scream or roar like a lion while you are dancing.

In the Trance Dance trainings we dance for 4½ days. Most

people do not realize or believe that they are going to dance that much, but when they go home after the training they are generally still dancing. And they dance for weeks after. They lose weight naturally, their skin begins to clear and brighten, their eyes clear. Physically and emotionally they transform because through movement and breath they are healing physically and emotionally.

We also heal mentally when we dance; when we dance in trance, we move into a state of consciousness where we envision, imagine, or see experiences which are stored in our far memory. We literally move as consciousness to that place or time which is a parallel reality to this life. We experience other places and times, not just witnessing, but actually participating in this non-ordinary place or time.

This clears out a lot of the petty thinking, a lot of fearful thoughts that cause us to worry, because when we get in touch with our immortality, there really is not much to worry about and crisis in this life remains in its proper perspective. The loss of a loved one does not devastate us; we feel sad because of their absence, but we don't allow it to wipe us out because we know that we have lost thousands of loved ones and we will be in love again.

The petty things that we worry about, the small things that build up, are the root causes of all disease, especially those diseases for which we have been unable to determine cures. Some people suffer so from this negative petty thinking that they have developed a chronic negative life plan.

When we were born our self-esteem was so high that some people had difficulty being around us, which is why they unconsciously 'stole our Spirit' and robbed us of our self-esteem. 'Soul theft' or having our Spirit stolen in our contemporary world refers to the loss of Spirit which occurs in painful intimate relationships between lovers, children, parents and so on. Every child is born enlightened with the high self-esteem that enlightenment brings. Every child feels loved, wants to love, demands to be loved. They don't cling to problems. They experience, express feelings and move on. Through adjustments to physical reality and because of our parents we become damaged. One of my teachers, Buckminster Fuller, said, 'We are all born creative, lovable geniuses and some of us were less damaged than others', meaning that we all were damaged in varying degrees.

Those life shocks and traumas of childhood need to be healed. Sometimes we even need to heal previous lives, both human and pre-human; deaths that were horrible, lives that were painful, patterns of rejection, suffering and denial during battles, famines, ice ages. Trance Dancing creates the possibility to travel beyond this time and space and heal these fossilized thoughts, events and shocks.

The Power of Spirit

To be disenchanted, to be dispirited, is to be diseased. I don't want you to get stuck in whether you believe in religion or not: that is irrelevant. Spirituality has nothing to do with religion and that is the mistake that many of us have made.

Religion is an organized system or path that you follow through the wisdom and enlightenment of a specific teacher, whether Jesus, Moses or Mohammed. Spirituality is not a one-prophet model. Spirituality requires that everybody be a prophet. Spirituality requires that every individual has their own connection to what they call God and what I have come to call Spirit.

The priest or the rabbi is only someone with the responsibility for the community's communication to God. The priest or rabbi is not responsible for your individual connection to God or Spirit unless employed by you, for you are already partially God and therefore for the priest to represent you is foolish. You don't need a priest to talk to God for you.

You instinctively knew this as a child. Just watch any child and watch the way they pray. They are not going through a middle person, they are not parroting prayers, they go directly to the Source because they know where they came from, they still have cognitive far memory. So, they talk directly to God. Then, as we grow older, we start reciting prayers, the meaning of which most of the time we don't even know. Eventually we get lost in dogma that threatens us with guilt if we have the courage to commune directly with Spirit.

It is only since the advent of science, which is relatively new when viewed within the entire context of our evolution, that we have begun to believe that we think with our brain. Before science, during Goddess and shamanic times, we believed we thought with our hearts. Thinking with our hearts is not such a radical idea when we realize that we do it when we choose to – when we help a child, when we support the disabled or unconditionally love our own child or lover.

What *is* true about the brain is that the brain is a receiver of thought like a radio receives stations, or a TV receives channels. The way to receive different thoughts is to change the way we think. This is done by moving beyond time and space through trance and tuning into an alternative vibration or thought form.

When we believe that we live in one reality, then we think in one way and our brains only receive one repetitive thought form, or channel. We then become a diseased and dispirited person who eventually loses their connection to Spirit and the insights of Spirit's domain. When we have the courage to change the way we think, we become confused. This is really a positive state of consciousness because this confusion means we are about to free our mind, to let go of old restricting beliefs and receive new insights which can only be received once we release the old conflicting beliefs which effectively block new ideas and perceptions.

Healing through placebo, which all of us accept but none

of us fully understands, is a good example of the power of thought. Many of the studies show that if the patient really believes that you are giving them a new miracle cure for a particular illness or disease, miraculously the disease somehow will disappear. This has worked with severe illnesses such as cancer. Specific cases are documented thoroughly by the work being done by many, such as Bernie Segal and the Simington Clinic in Dallas/Fortworth, Texas, USA. The Simingtons have done extensive research on the effects of placebo. The Stendig Clinic for children with cancer, in Houston, Texas, also often uses visualization and placebos. Belief in a new miracle cure is the same as the belief in Spirit who provides the new insights and understanding which occur during Trance Dancing.

So there is something very powerful in believing we are connected with Spirit or a form of energy, Goddess, God, consciousness, or intelligence, call it what you will, and when believed it somehow heals us. Dancing has traditionally always been an invitation to Spirit to come into our body. It is only in the last hundred years that we have come to believe that dance is only a form of recreation. We have taken too many things from our ancestors like dance, sex, teaching plants, hunting and turned them into just recreation. In the past Trance Dancing was an opportunity not just for recreation, but actually to re-create ourselves spiritually and therefore heal ourselves through the presence of Spirit.

In only a few parts of the world was dancing for recreation. In the South Pacific the Hula societies were shamans; their idea of shamanism was entertainment. They would travel from village to village, sing, dance, massage, lift the Spirits of people and then they would move on. That was their magic. But for the most part in other cultures, dance occurred in rituals and therefore had a very sacred purpose.

Similarly, we now also use psychoactive herbs and other plants for recreation. Again, our ancestors never did this just for recreation. They did it for the specific purpose of going into a trance state, to contact Spirit animals, to look into the future so that they could see what their life was going to be like and create it, to look into their past so that they could see the evolution of their consciousness and gain the confidence of their immortality. These herbs, plants and mushrooms were all considered gifts from Spirit, spiritual sacraments, and were never viewed as drugs. We must go beyond our conditioned fear of these plants, embrace their wisdom and healing power. We must once again assume our responsibility as the elders of humanity and teach people how to use these plants as our wise ancestors did, to bring clarity and insight to the rites of passage of our lives.

4 How to Trance Dance

Getting Started

The most important thing I can tell you about how to Trance Dance is that it is a matter of *trusting the process*, of just doing it and allowing Spirit to embody you, causing you to awaken a full and whole sense of who you truly are physically and metaphysically.

Preparing for your first Trance Dance session can be a bit frightening for some. Please realize that this fear will transform to excitement once you begin to experience your own dancer within. If you're working on your own, rather than in a group or workshop, be assured: there is nothing to be afraid of and the music will be your inspiration and guide. Wear clothes that you like and feel good in, and that allow you to move comfortably, clothes that you can remove easily should you feel so inclined while dancing.

Be sure to have a bandanna. This is a piece of cloth worn around the forehead and pulled down over the eyes. It's usually colourful with designs and symbols that communicate various messages. Your bandanna should express who you are. At the very least you need a blindfold, but this is more impersonal – just a device to keep out light.

Also, eat lightly. It is much easier to move around when you don't have a full stomach.

If you are accustomed to wearing make-up, you might want to consider wearing less or none at all as your face and body will sweat. This choice, though, is up to you.

Dancing barefoot is best, but if the surface does not allow this, consider wearing some kind of soft foot protection. Dancing barefoot is especially good outdoors on the earth, not just for aesthetic reasons but because the Spirit energy of Mother Earth will flow uninhibited into your body.

Unless they are power objects (see page 20) remove heavy belts, large rings, earrings and other forms of jewellery, to protect you and also to protect the people that you are dancing with. Remove anything that touches your body in a such a way that it reminds you that you have a body. Attention determines reality and the less attention on your body the better.

Be sure to have by you power objects for those times afterwards when you integrate your experiences through writing and talking. Also consider having with you your favourite blanket to create a sacred space to lie down on after your dance.

Also, I suggest you come drug free to your initial Trance Dance experience. At some point, if you choose to use teacher plants, this is okay but you will find that it is not really necessary as – once awakened by Spirit – images, feelings, smells, tastes, sounds and thoughts of other times will flow freely.

When Trance Dancing, you do not really need a great deal of space. Trance Dancing does not need a lot of space because the dance is really happening within.

Before you begin, check on pages 43–4 that you aren't one of the people who shouldn't be Trance Dancing. Don't worry: there aren't that many of them.

Your eyes should be closed and covered with a bandanna,

your feet firmly planted upon Mother Earth or the floor of the space within which you are dancing. Your feet should be shoulder-width apart. Your knees are slightly bent to allow passionate energy to flow up through you; your belly is let out; your chest falls in softly; shoulders drop; arms and hands just hang and your head floats upon your neck.

Allow your head to move slightly and begin to breathe deeply using the 'Breath of Fire' of two inhales through the nose and one exhale through the mouth (see page 58), or any other conscious breath pattern which causes you to fill your entire lungs with air rich in oxygen and energy. The conscious breathing should go on for a minimum of three to five minutes and *should* take place before the music starts, but it's OK if it's done with the beginning of the music.

During this time you allow your body to move according to the thoughts and emotions that begin to emerge within you. If sounds are there, feel free to release them. If tears occur, see them as 'healing rain' which is cleansing you. Sounds of joy, laughter, pain, fear and sadness are all appropriate, so long as they are coming from within and not coming from your ego in search of attention from the other dancers.

At some point you will feel a vibration or passionate energy moving through your body which will cause involuntary movements. This is usually an indication that you have begun to evoke Spirit and that Spirit is now beginning to embody you. At that point the dancer becomes the dance and the Energizer within you is awakened. When this happens there is usually no conscious control of the body and your consciousness moves beyond the limitations of time and space. Your body may also realize a new form or a very ancient one (see Chapter 7) much in the same way your shamanic ancestors would transform into Spirit animals while Trance Dancing.

You will experience profound emotions, joyous ones and

even those that you would normally consider negative. When these occur you will usually 'bilocate', so at the same time that you are experiencing these negative emotions, you are also present, observing and witnessing them. This brings a sense of peace and security that you generally do not experience when you are in normal reality and at the mercy of your emotions.

Spirit animals, aspects of nature, tribal rituals, all may appear before you, and you may experience pains in particular parts of your body associated with past injuries from this life and former lives, the details of which may be either clear or unknown to you.

All of this will occur in a very short time. A 45-minute dance is usually enough time to move into deep trance.

Is Trance Dancing for Everyone?

As much as I would like to believe that Trance Dancing is for everybody, it seems not to be the case. It comes more easily to some than others and, for those who are excessively cognitive, it can be extremely difficult.

If you are a member of or have a background or interest in cultures which used Trance Dance, it probably will come more easily to you and may even make rational sense to you. However, for many people from North America and Europe, the thought of doing Trance Dancing may create discomfort or a feeling that this is a very bizarre thing to be involved in. This may particularly be the case if you are, like I was, an urban person living in one of our major cities who had allowed most of his life to take place in that part of his body that rests above the shoulders and between the ears.

Trance Dance may be especially difficult for those of us who have allowed ourselves to become slaves to time, machines and the consensus reality. Many of us have become victims of our left-brain logic and have stress-related disorders. If this describes you, as it did me, at least try Trance Dancing. It is a great adventure and an opportunity to meet a part of yourself which has been diseased and dormant for lifetimes. You may even gain some insight into and appreciation for other cultures as I did for the North American Indians. I initially dismissed their culture as something which had lost its relevance to contemporary life. I now realize how ignorant I was. Since Trance Dancing has become part of my life, the 'Spirit dancer' within me has shown a deep appreciation for their culture and perceptions of life.

Cautions

Beyond the cultural considerations, there are a few physical considerations which may restrict your involvement in Trance Dancing.

1 *Epilepsy.* People with epilepsy are discouraged from being involved in Trance Dancing because of the possibly seizure-producing conditions which are generated by some of the music and movement.
2 *Cardiovascular disorders.* Individuals with *severe* cardiovascular problems are also discouraged from being involved with Trance Dancing because the rapid and forceful dances might aggravate their condition. If you are capable of listening to your body and slowing it when it speaks to you, Trance Dancing may still be for you.
3 *Pregnancy.* Women in their first trimester of pregnancy are encouraged to wait until later in their pregnancy or until after the child's birth before Trance Dancing.
4 *Menstruation.* Women in early stages of menstruation should be advised of the possible flow increases and dizziness that may occur during Trance Dance.

Psychological Considerations

Trance Dancing is not recommended for individuals with a history of severe psychotic disorders. On the other hand, if you have experienced some mild depressions as we all have and if you are neurotic like the rest of humanity, Trance Dancing will work better for you than most classical therapy.

If you have great difficulty in letting go and allowing your unconscious to flow freely, there are other forms of healing, such as meditation, massage, breath work (pranayama), or any other form of relaxation, that will support your Trance Dancing.

Spiritual Considerations

Although the roots of Trance Dance are in ancient spiritual practices and belief systems, Trance Dance itself has no particular religious orientation and need not be seen as being in competition with your own religious views. Be clear though that many Trance Dancers report experiences that for them have significant spiritual meaning. Usually these experiences include an increase in one's appreciation of a higher power and the acknowledgement of one's own spiritual nature. Many people come to Trance Dance seeking these experiences but just as many are ecstatically surprised once their conditioned scepticism transforms into extraordinary spiritual experience.

Positive Results

Now that I have cautioned you about Trance Dancing, I would like to share some of the positive results individuals have experienced:

- A direct experience and trust in the metaphysical healing powers we all possess
- Healing through disappearance of lifelong patterns of disease-oriented behaviour
- An increase in the trust that Spirit is real and not just a concept or dogmatic tradition
- A leap into the adventure of exploring oneself without judgement or making oneself wrong
- The wisdom which comes once you realize your immortality, which usually manifests in taking responsibility for your life
- A reduction of ego which is replaced by a willingness to appreciate and support others
- A pleasurable relaxation into just going with the experiences of life
- Incredible energy, excitement and aliveness
- The healing of breath-related illness such as asthma, and other illnesses such as rheumatism and arthritis
- The awakening of a personal Energizer and a return to deep, satisfying, guiltless sex
- An increased ability to see visual phenomena and the movement of energy in everything
- A greater awareness of one's inner world
- A general lightness, resulting from satisfaction and well-being
- The experience of one's body and physical form changing from this time to other times, from human to non-human
- Perceptions dramatically transformed, the dancer often describing having entered another world; some experience Goddesses, Gods, Spirit animals and teachers and others experience being the stars of the universe.

Countless dancers have said that they perceive life with a new significance and they themselves begin to take on new behaviours and ultimately a new form. Dancers also report that when they go deeply into trance, they become the drum or the music itself. They experience no separation and become one with everything.

Trance Dance obviously induces many altered states of consciousness but this requires the dancer to let go of conscious control. The use of the Breath of Fire (see pages 58–61) and other conscious breathing patterns encourages letting go. This is usually followed by a tingling through the entire body. The most commonly reported psychic phenomenon is far memory or archaic memories. It is not uncommon at all for dancers to report having regressed back to earlier times when they were part of a primitive ritual or rite of passage, and some even move back to times before they had a human form. People with no knowledge of Spirit animals find themselves being visited by or embodied by an animal consciousness, and while dancing begin to take on the personality and qualities of that animal (see Chapter 7).

Please realize that the experiences reported by dancers vary greatly from person to person and from dance to dance. However, these results are often seen after only one session.

Dancers often will begin to move as animals or warriors and quite often women will re-enact experiences of giving birth. Many will re-enact being sacrificed in a ritual. While dancing, some will experience killing or being killed; others will experience the 'final passage' into death. When the dancer has experienced deep emotional releases, they sometimes continue seeing the same scenes with their eyes open for a short time following the dance.

None of this should alarm you in any way. It's highly unlikely that you will ever experience anything you cannot deal with. When you are in trance the psyche splits, so you are simultaneously witnessing the recall or memory even as you are experiencing it. There is no pain in present time; you may be surprised or vulnerable because of the uniqueness of an experience, but you will not be overwhelmed.

If you are dancing on your own, it's extremely improbable that in a dance of 45 to 90 minutes you'll reach such a deep state that you would have difficulty coming to terms with any of your experiences. To get deeply into trance, people usually need help and encouragement, as it's a state that the Western brain resists. In group training sessions, deeper trance is possible and desirable, but if you're dancing on your own you needn't worry that you're going to end up somewhere you don't want to be.

 # 5 How Trance Dance Works and How It Feels

Before we move on to look at breathing in more detail, this short chapter will just outline what might be going on physically when we Trance Dance and also what is happening on a spiritual level.

Endorphins

The theory of why trance is induced, at least initially, has to do with endorphins. Endorphins are neuro-hormones or substances highly similar in structure and function to opiates. They are generated in the body and are released under various conditions, such as pain, stress, acupuncture, sex, long distance running and Trance Dancing.

Within contemporary endorphin science there is a theory that endorphins are also released in states of spiritual embodiment and during high energy dancing. In the 1980 conference on 'Shamans and Endorphins' it was reported that 'hypnotic analgesia and endorphin-based analgesia result from drum and dance activity and that the powerful visions or dream states that occur through Trance Dancing may activate both hypnotic and endorphin analgesia'. In other words, the music, the dancing and the trance all create feelings of ecstasy.

Being Present

When you identify yourself as a body rather than a Spirited being, you will search naively for 'out of body' experiences. Trance Dancing does not work like this. It invites Spirit to *return home* to the body which makes you more Spirited. You merge with your greater self and become so filled with Spirit that your body is no longer your primary focus and identification. You then experience being one with the Universal Spirit or what TNI calls the 'Incomprehensible Collective Consciousness'.

Through Trance Dancing you are filled with Spirit, whole and present. This is the opposite to an out of body experience.

Being spirited or present means you become so filled with Spirit that it fills you totally until you overflow, so that you connect with the incomprehensible. This feels like you are out of your body, because you identify yourself as Spirit or energy rather than just a body.

When this is done with other dancers your individual Spirits merge and a conscious collective orgasm occurs. (This occurs at the level of 'energy', although many people do experience individual physical orgasm too.) Energy, endorphins, organic opiates and healing energies are set free; a channel is opened up to the life-giving powers and a vital energizing takes place. The more dancers, the more Spirit; the more Spirit, the more energy; the more energy, the more intense the spiritual orgasm.

 **6 The Power of Breath**

Why Breath is Important

Breath is the physical form of Spirit. When you alter breath, you alter consciousness. When you alter consciousness, your breath changes.

Life is dependent upon active breathing. To breathe is to live. To breathe is to be consciously alive. Without breath there is no life. Humans are dependent upon breath for their life and for their health. Other animals must also breathe to live; even plants breathe and are dependent on air for their continued life and existence.

Life is a series of breaths from that first small faint breath we take as an infant to that last gasp on our deathbed. The story of life is the continuation of breath. Breathing is the most important function of all functions of the body, for all the other functions depend upon it. We can exist for some time without eating, a shorter time without drinking, but without breathing our existence is reduced to a matter of minutes.

The breathing patterns that we teach during Trance Dance events are not only vital to inducing a trance state of consciousness, but they will lengthen your days upon this earth by giving you increased vitality and the power to resist disease and toxins. The opposite is also true; careless breathing will tend to shorten your life, decrease your vitality and cause you to be vulnerable to disease.

As we become more civilized, we learn to breathe in a less effective way as regards our health and vitality.

The connection between correct breathing, altered states of consciousness and vital health is easy to see. One of the consistent results of Trance Dancing is that the participants report a new sense of vitality and well-being. Their sleeping patterns change; they have more energy and need less physical rest. Often they even report that chronic illnesses and fatigue disappear. Be clear that what is doing this is not just the physical movement involved in dancing but also the increased amount of conscious breathing which occurs while dancing.

In addition to the physical benefits, breathing properly also improves mental powers, shifts one's emotions from low to high and increases a sense of clear-sightedness and control over the physical reality in which we live. Spiritual growth is also increased.

Air contains more than oxygen, hydrogen and nitrogen. Something far more important and magical occurs in conscious breathing than just an increased amount of oxygen in the blood. While dancing the Trance Dancer is embodied by Spirit. Spirit moves in and out of the Trance Dancer's physical form with their breathing. This rhythmic breathing brings the dancer into harmonious vibration with nature and causes the dancer's enchantment, powers and visions of other realities. The elimination of disease and the removal of negative emotions, such as fear and worry, are also promoted by spirited breath.

If you do not breathe a sufficient quantity of air, the work of the blood cannot go on properly and the result is that the body is insufficiently nourished and cleansed. Impurities manifest in some form of disease. Lack of sufficient oxygen means poor nutrition, poor elimination and bad health.

When one breathes in a shallow way, which is the way most people in the civilized world have been conditioned to breathe, only a part of the lungs are used and a great portion of the lung capacity is lost.

Animals, indigenous people and our primitive ancestors breathed differently from us. When we go into breathing patterns which move us into trance, we are in many ways returning to the way our primitive ancestors breathed all the time. This method of breathing, although lost in the civilized world, is easily accomplished through Trance Dancing.

Esoteric teachers of all times and lands have taught that there was to be found in the air a substance from which all activity, vitality and life was derived, although they differed in their names for this force. The most well-known name for this force is the Sanskrit *prana* which means absolute energy or 'the universal principle of energy or force'.

When I am teaching Trance Dance presenters, I make it clear to the trainees that through the breath patterns I teach, they will acquire an increase of energy. Energy is my word for *prana*.

Energy is the power that breathes life into all created form, the element from which all activity, vitality and life are derived, the universal force.

Consider *prana* as the active principle of life, the vital energy or vital force that creates continuous life. It is found in all forms of life from amoeba to human, from the most elementary form of plant life to the highest form of animal life. *Prana* or energy is all pervading. It is found in all things having life and, as esoteric philosophies teach, life is in all things, in every atom, in every molecule. The lifelessness of some things and some people is only a lesser amount of *prana* or energy; therefore, energy is everywhere and in everything and everything is alive.

Through Trance Dancing you can tap into this energy; it is the easiest way I have discovered in 30 years to receive this energy. This energy can also be called Spirit; the Spirit of life. In the Hebrew book of Genesis they refer to it as 'the breath of the Spirit of life'. This energy is in atmospheric air and it is also elsewhere. It can penetrate where the air cannot go. The oxygen in air sustains animal life. The carbon in air sustains plant life. Energy is responsible for the manifestation and creation of all life.

We are constantly inhaling air charged with energy and extracting from it this energy and using it. Energy is found in its freest form in atmospheric air which when fresh is highly charged with this force. We draw it to us more easily from air than from any other source. When we are Trance Dancing we draw greater amounts of energy into the body, which manifests as vitality, health, humour, laughter, playfulness, enthusiasm, excitement and all other positive emotions. In ordinary breathing we absorb a normal supply of energy, but through Trance Dancing or other forms of conscious breathing, we extract from the air a greater supply of energy which is stored away in the brain and nerve centres to be used when we need it. We store away energy just as a battery stores electricity.

The many powers of spiritual teachers are the result of their knowledge of how to extract energy from the air, how to store it and how to use it intelligently. One who has acquired the skill of storing away energy often radiates vitality and strength, which is felt by those coming into contact with them. They can pass on their vitality, effecting what we call 'spontaneous healing'. This occurs quite often in our Trance Dances. We transmit this vitality in such a subtle and simple way that often the person does not realize that their disease has gone. Because the body's natural state is one of harmony and health, people often miss bringing attention to the fact that their discomfort has disappeared.

Just as oxygen from the air is used by the blood in the circulatory system, the energy in the air is used by the brain and nervous system. As oxygenated blood is carried to all parts of the circulatory system, stored energy is also carried to all parts of the nervous system, adding strength and vitality.

Just as the oxygen in the blood is used up by the needs of that system, so the supply of energy taken up by the nervous system is exhausted by our thinking, willing, acting and processing. Therefore the energy needs constant replenishing. Every thought, every act, every effort of will, every motion of a muscle uses up a certain amount of energy. Once you understand the relationship between the air that you inhale and the amount of energy which is stored in your nervous system to sustain and vitalize life, the importance of breathing is easily understood. Therefore the value of Trance Dancing which causes healthy breathing to occur naturally is easy to appreciate.

With Trance Dancing one begins to move and breathe naturally in a healthy way. No discipline is really required, just the willingness to enjoy dancing, feel, breathe and live.

Nose versus Mouth Breathing

We teach the Breath of Fire and other forms of conscious breathing to our students to encourage them to breathe more regularly through their nose, rather than continue the bad habit of mouth breathing, which many of us in the modern civilized world suffer from. Learning how to breathe through the nostrils and to overcome the common practice of mouth breathing can transform the way in which we experience ourselves and our health. Practitioners of Eastern medicine have long believed that nostril breathing brings health and strength. Mouth breathing is useful sometimes to break up and release emotions, but the constant habit of mouth breathing brings disease and weakness.

Your organs of respiration have their first protection and filter in the nostrils. When the breath is taken through the mouth there is one fewer protection to catch the dust and other toxins in the air.

The nostrils also perform an important function in warming the air being inhaled, so that it can do no damage to the delicate organs of the throat and lungs. When you breathe through your nose the air that enters the lungs is as different from the outside air as distilled water is from water from the tap. Breathing through your mouth makes as much sense as eating food through your nose. No animals except humans sleep with their mouth open or breathe through their mouth.

The nose is the only orifice in the human body that has direct passage to the brain. When breathing in a conscious way, such as the Breath of Fire, we inhale not only oxygen but also energy that goes directly to the brain. This creates a sense of euphoria or trance which, through movement, is further enhanced by the natural secretion of endorphins in the brain.

The Breath of Fire

The Breath of Fire is the name that I gave to a particular pattern of breathing, because it creates transformative consciousness and fire is the element of transformation. Fire is the element in which Spirit lives, meaning that there are physical life forms in air and earth and sea. But the only life form that can survive the flame is non-physical and spiritual.

The breath pattern that I recommend that you use is the Breath of Fire. Make two inhalations through the nose and one exhalation through the mouth. It can be done slowly or rapidly. Obviously, when you do it in a more rapid pattern you are going to take in more oxygen and energy. This will alter your consciousness. Some of you may feel a tingling sensation and maybe even a slight paralysis in your arms and hands. A Tibetan monk doesn't call this hyperventilation, he calls it trance. Tibetan monks breathe that way for days, go into trance, pass out, have water splashed on them, re-awaken, breathe and go into trance again. They don't die from it, they don't have heart attacks from it, and that is because they don't believe that is what will happen. They believe it is a spiritual practice that alters their consciousness allowing them to travel beyond space and time. I recommend that you approach it with this same understanding.

If you find this idea worrying, let me reassure you. The problem is that people are literally afraid of breathing. I have done this work for over 35 years, have had no problems, no serious side effects. All have emerged from this experience purged of lethargy and inertia, filled with health, excitement and passion. It's been done with the elderly, children, corporate executives and the non-initiated. There is nothing to worry about. Relax, and breathe!

If you do get worried about the breathing, it says something about your participation and activity in life, for breath is life. When breathing, hold your breath, taking in more oxygen and energy. When this is done regularly you maintain a condition of health superior to the average person. You are more energetic, more alive. Listlessness and fatigue disappear. The boredom which accompanies the mundane duties of life also disappears. You become more animated, more energetic, more alive and therefore you attract similar vibrations in the form of friends, lovers, entertainment, work, thoughts and emotions.

There are basically two forms of breath known to the average person: high or shallow breathing, where the air located in our lower respiratory system is never circulated, and low or deep breathing, where more of the air is replenished. High breathing is the worst form of breathing known and requires the greatest use of energy. It is energy wasting and has little or no benefit. It is quite common in the civilized world and many persons who breathe in this way become addicted to mouth breathing. In low or deep breathing the lungs are given a freer play and consequently more air is inhaled.

The trouble with both these methods is that in neither of them do the lungs become totally filled with air. High breathing fills only the upper portion of the lungs, low breathing fills only the lower and middle parts of the lungs. Any method which will fill the entire lung space enables you to absorb the greatest quantity of oxygen and to store away the greatest amount of energy.

The Breath of Fire includes all the good points of high breathing and low breathing. It brings into play the entire respiratory system, every part of the lungs, every cell and every respiratory muscle. The maximum amount of benefit is derived from the minimum amount of energy use. One of the most important features of the Breath of Fire is the fact that the respiratory muscles are called fully into play, whereas in other forms of breathing only a portion of these muscles are used. I recommend that you practise the Breath of Fire before you begin to use it while dancing. This will allow you to have a more conscious understanding of the optimal effective way to do it.

Method

1 Stand or sit erect, breathing through your nostrils and just inhale steadily, first filling the lower part of your lungs. This brings into play your diaphragm and pushes forward the front walls of your abdomen. Then begin to fill the middle part of your lungs, pushing out the lower ribs and chest. Then fill the higher portion of the lungs, pushing out the upper chest, thus lifting the chest including the upper six or seven pairs of ribs.

When you first do this, it appears as if these are three separate movements; this however, is not the case. The inhalation is continuous. The entire chest cavity from the lower diaphragm to the highest point of the chest are being expanded in one uniform movement.

This is why in the Breath of Fire I ask you to take two inhalations through the nose, thus guaranteeing that you draw in enough air to fill the entire lungs. Eventually, with practice, you will not even need the two inhalations, although I recommend that you continue to use them until one long continuous breath is sufficient.

2 You should retain the breath for one or two seconds.
3 Exhale slowly through the nose or, as we sometimes recommend, through the mouth. Exhaling slowly through the mouth enables you to make a sound which is also a way of releasing emotions.

Energy Breathing

The sage Bhagvan Patanjali, father of yoga philosophy, said:

Those who have control over their inner 'prana' [energy] can store it in their system and use it to heal others by mentally transmitting a portion of this supply to those in need. By their touch alone these people can cure many ailments.

Through energy breathing you can acquire about seven times the normal quantity of oxygen and energy. This means supercharging the blood with oxygen and the brain with energy. Richness of the blood is the basis of the entire body's health and the blood can be called rich only if it contains the necessary amount of oxygen and nutrition. Supercharging the nervous system and brain with energy expands consciousness, transforms reality and heals psychological pain and fatigue.

The following are types of energy breathing you can use either when dancing or at other times to ensure that you are storing superior amounts of energy.

Deep Breathing

Exhale slowly, then inhale slowly. Expand the stomach and then the chest to allow the maximum amount of air in. As the chest becomes full don't hold the breath, but exhale slowly. In both inhalation and exhalation the breath should be one continuous flow.

Repeat this breathing slowly and steadily. This method fills the lungs to capacity and empties them thoroughly. This method is especially good for those who smoke any kind of tobacco, teacher plants, or herbs and those who work in environments where there may be a greater amount of toxins in the air.

Energy Breath

Energy Breath is the breath pattern I was taught by my spiritual Master, Baba Muktananda. It is the breath pattern through which he taught me to initiate *shaktipat*, or transmit energy from my body to someone else's. It has been used for hundreds of years and is taught in yoga classes around the world.

You do rapid inhalations and exhalations, alternating the two forcefully as many times as you can handle. There is no retention of air, giving equal force to both the exhalation and the inhalation, until you reach the point where you cannot go any further.

At that point stop, giving slight extra force to the exhalation. When you have finished exhaling completely, take a long slow inhalation filling the lungs as much as possible, and hold that breath. While that breath is being held, you will experience a tingling in your body. Retain the breath as long as you can, then exhale the breath evenly through the nose or mouth.

This is one round of Energy Breath. You continue to do round after round until your body is so filled with energy that not only does the tingling begin to move to the extremities of your hands and your feet, but you also begin to feel a tingling in your brain. Continue to do round after round until at the final exhalation of a round, you feel your body thrusting you backward. That is the signal that your body has become filled totally with energy and you have connected with Spirit. You will fall and go into an instantaneous state of deep trance.

The benefits are that you are able to transmit energy from your body to someone else's, that you move into a deep void, the deepest form of trance which is the absence of thought entirely. It also brings heat to the body when it is cold, helps to cure asthma, improves digestion and stimulates the entire body quickly when it suffers from fatigue or tiredness.

Spirit Breath

Once you have practised Energy Breath and feel that it comes very naturally to you, you can increase its potency and power by contracting the sphincter muscles situated at the rectum during that part of the breath pattern when you are holding your breath. While holding your breath suck the entire rectum upward and hold it. When done effectively you will feel a rush of energy moving upward from its normal downward course, moving up through the spine, through the neck and exploding in the head. Spirit Breath eventually empowers you to speed up the process of transmutation of energy from atmospheric air to you and from you to whomever you choose to transmit it. (Transmutation is the genetic change which goes on at cellular level in all life forms.)

7 *Spirit Animals*

The Importance of Animals

All people everywhere have a profound need for animals and there is no substitute for them. Animals have played a significant role in forming our speech and thought. They were the first visitors to our 'mind's eye' and they played an indispensable role in our becoming human.

In our early years, we see animals directly without interpretation or symbolism – they are horse, bird and elephant – they are all part of nature. As children, we actively pretend to be them and we give them names. Animal to animal, they teach us to feel and behave, to assume attitudes and personalities.

As children, we speak to animals and they to us. It is through these non-ordinary-reality conversations that we learn to relate to and eventually bond to the earth. As children we travel to many places, all of which are abundant with bears, frogs, rabbits and other magical animals.

We learn about transformation from the snake who sheds its skin, the frog who loses its tail and grows legs, or the butterfly who has metamorphosed from the caterpillar. By interacting with animals we prepare for our own transformations and rites of passage, such as leaving home, marriage, sex and choice of a spiritual path. As we grow older we realize that transformation is a major part of life and in fact maybe the prime indicator of 'aliveness'.

As we learn to play with animals we begin to dance, which is really our rhythmic imitation of animals.

We acquire a dance style of our own by copying the movements of birds, mammals, reptiles and creatures of other evolutionary stages – we 'dance our animal'. As we become more adult we realize that certain animals are the keepers of important mysteries, such as metamorphosis, birth, puberty, healing, courtship, fertility and defence. By dancing these animals, these secrets come into our understanding and are realized as power, which is why our shamanic ancestors called certain animals 'power animals'.

Everyone has at least one 'power animal' who awaits their discovery beyond space/time. After encountering our power animal or animals we can bring its mystery and its power back to our ordinary reality.

Dancing your animal regularly ensures that the power remains embodied within you.

The most popular Spirit animal in the northern hemisphere is the bear. The bear is so powerful that it has changed the evolution of human consciousness. The brown bear's size, appearance, mobility, dexterity, reproduction, annual cycle, length of life, social behaviour and intelligence all have an undeniable relationship with ours. Across America, Europe, Asia, Mexico, the Mediterranean and the Himalayas for over 50 millennia the bear has been celebrated in festivals as sacred messenger, meditator, hunter, grandparent, teacher and traveller between worlds.

The bear, like us, has a versatile style: exploratory, pushy, relentless, analytical and risk taking. Bears fish, hunt, pick berries and gather honey. They have an expressive face, three-dimensional vision and vocal and gestural responses. They sit and can walk on rear feet, have almost no tail and great dexterity. In winter the brown bear withdraws into the earth. This winter sleep coincides with our winter withdrawal and search for self. When the bear emerges from this winter of sleep and introspection, spring emerges and abundant life returns. This cycle or rhythm of life represented death and rebirth to our ancestors. Later, when religions were formed, the bear was worshipped. Bear madonnas still exist throughout the world. The Bear is the keeper of the gates of life and death, this world and other worlds, flesh and Spirit, human and animal form, inside and outside. Bear is the mediator between man and woman, the natural and the sacred. The Bear as Spirit guide predates all the human guides to other worlds – shamans, Orpheus, Jesus, the Holy Mother.

Replacing the bear and other Spirit animals with the human figure deprives us of our sacred power, substituting for it faith and belief. This loss causes us to work through spiritual middlemen and makes us deaf to our animal brothers and sisters who speak within us. Our failure to hear the wisdom of our Spirit animal is a failure to be fully initiated into human life.

Dancing our Spirit animal existed before yoga. Yoga positions have been copied from animal movements. Most of them received names from animals, like lion, cobra, dog and fish. Yoga reawakens the consciousness and quality of the animal, while practising that animal's position.

When we allow ourselves to be natural, we remain true to the world of nature. We are in awe of wild animals and we know that words cannot replace dancing our animal for when we do they speak to us with incredible wisdom. No words will ever replace our participation in the dances and rituals which honour these beasts, our ancestors. They are our kindred spirits, we were thought up by them. Before humans were born, they worked out life in thousands of variations, they led the way and showed us how to awaken our consciousness. We are members of the human family, but dancing our Spirit animal enlarges our perception beyond the limits of being human and allows us to enter the wisdom of lizard, monkey and fish.

Dancing Your Animal

Shamans believed that they were related to animals thousands of years before Charles Darwin put forward his theories of evolution. They can talk with their Spirit animal and can metamorphose into the form of their animal. The Christian Church considered those who could metamorphose to be wizards, witches and sorcerers and persecuted them.

Dancing accompanied by drumming was used to experience being embodied by a Spirit animal. The dancer would observe the animal's personality and movements, and gesture, leap and yell to their Spirit animal's consciousness. The use of masks and other body decorations such as feathers made moving past imitation to actual embodiment possible.

When dancing your animal use recorded music (for example, Professor Trance's *Shaman's Breath* CD), drumming, rattles, appropriate animal movements and sounds such as bird calls, growls and roars. You will then move beyond imitating your animal to actually being embodied by the power of your animal.

To dance your animal, move freely, picking up the feeling of any animal at first until one begins to be more strongly present than the others. When this happens, focus your energy on becoming that animal. Experience the emotions of that animal, make its sounds aloud. Look within your mind's eye at the animal's environment or maybe even see the animal itself. In a trance state you can bilocate and simultaneously both be and see the animal. If it seems right, begin to move more quickly as the animal. For example, let's say you are feeling the presence of a deer. Think about how a deer behaves in the wild, the alert head looking for danger, the head reaching down to eat grass, freezing at the first sign of danger and then running like the wind to escape.

When you have completed dancing your animal, welcome its Spirit by stopping dancing and expressing your gratitude for its power having returned home to your body.

After you have danced your animal a few times, you may want to use a teacher plant to pump up the experience. To maintain the power of your Spirit animal you must dance your animal regularly. Even when this is done, eventually that Spirit animal will move on, allowing you to have many during your life. I have even had as many as three at one time. The black panther who represented my emotional body, the bear my mind and the eagle my Spirit. Going into nature or the wilderness also helps to satisfy your Spirit animal and causes you to come into your animal presence more easily.

There is no reason to ever be without a Spirit animal, for even when it is time for them to move on, they will usually introduce you to the Spirit animal whose power you need next in your life.

8 Masks, Mandalas and Rituals

Masks

Mask making is one of the spiritual practices which complement Trance Dancing. Only when wearing the mask is the dancer allowed to open his eyes and look out at the masks and movements of other dancers.

During the Trance Dance Presenters' training we usually require everyone to make a mask. This allows you really to express who you are at that time in your life, transcending your own personality and form. The mask allows you to become anyone and anything you choose to be.

After making the mask, it is important to wear it a few times before you actually dance and move in it.

Standing in front of a mirror to see and move like the personality of the mask is essential to actually becoming that animal, person, aspect of nature, or Spirit. However, it is undermining to wear a mask and walk around with it on while coming from your normal personality. You must think of the mask as a 'sacred reality' and only wear it when you intend to disappear into trance and become its power personality and Spirit.

Spend time making the mask. Talk to it, allow it to speak to you. Allow the mask to be magical, to become sacred.

When you perceive the mask as a powerful sacred object, its aliveness and power will compel you to become it when you wear it.

After you have talked to your mask and allowed it to tell you stories, stand in front of a mirror and demonstrate its power and wisdom by moving your arms, legs and feet. Move every part of your body, noticing which movements are motivated by the mask; use your voice and energy until all movement, sound and emotion conform to the attitude of the mask, until you disappear and portray the true character of the mask.

You must raise your awareness, lifting your energy source into your eyes until you see as the personality of the mask sees. Then allow the muscles of your entire body to relax as the mask's vision extends, connecting your entire body with the Spirit of the mask.

The Spirit of the mask must embody you and take over your entire form until you move and feel absent from your conscious physical form. The Spirit of the mask will reach out, moving your outstretched fingers, legs and head; allow the Spirit of the mask to take over, get out of your head, and feel the flow of the mask's energy rippling through you.

As each of Spirit's movements complete, your awareness will move beyond your physical form until you disappear into the immensity of Spirit's consciousness. The power of the mask will then come from within; you will lower your centre of gravity and become grounded in your earthbound animal nature. You cannot understand the power of mask Trance Dancing with your brain alone. As you move, hesitate every once in a while for an instant to witness the magic of your movement. Then let go and return to the adventure the mask creates for you.

While dancing, be sure to breathe deeply, allowing Spirit's breath to follow the rhythm of the music. Continue to lift, sway, and breathe to the rhythm until the music ends or the mask's Spirit leaves you.

Do this in front of a full-length mirror at least three times before you actually do the sacred mask dance with others. Also, if appropriate, we suggest that you do this one time in an altered state of consciousness using 'teacher plants' or 'the flesh of the Gods', but only do this after you have successfully experienced the dance in your natural state.

Making a Mask

The creative process of mask making requires you to access those spaces inside yourself where your information on 'how to create' lies. It is good to use music to help to align the two hemispheres of the brain. (TNI produce suitable tapes – see page 110.) You also need a physical space where the creative processes are respected and supported.

No previous skills are needed: the right portion of your brain will be the instrument to tap into imagination and the left portion will support you with analytical knowledge about the materials needed to create and assemble your mask. I believe everyone has these abilities. I believe everyone has made a mask at least once, if not in this life, then in a previous one. I will give you a few suggestions for the first time to support you in awakening and trusting your own abilities.

Begin by placing yourself in your sacred space. Sacred ground or space is created whenever we recognize and invoke the sacred or Spirit in that space, temple, home or landscape. The sacred is where illusions die and denial cracks open, where seeds sprout and light shoots forth. It is a place where awakening occurs and superior intelligence speaks, where the sacred calls us back to our true nature. In shamanism we can freely choose to make something or someone sacred, someone or something which is worthy of our sacrifice such as child, family, home. It's the open acknowledgement that there are things and people so valuable to us that we are willing to let go of our own desires and needs for the good of the greater relationship to person or place. There are sacred places like the great cathedrals and temples, divine places created by nature like mountains, waterfalls and canyons, and simple altars we create in our homes to honour Spirit.

Make sure your sacred space is free of distractions, then let yourself connect with your imagination and ask for your mask to come to you. When the image is clear and complete, draw it on paper. If you cannot visualize it, simply start to draw it. Lines and forms will flow from your hand to the paper and they will 'ring the bell' of your personal imagination.

When you are ready to choose the materials for your mask, consider the following.

The *base* of the mask needs to be made of healthy and resistant material because it is going to be in contact with your skin (you will breathe and sweat in it) and will have to withstand movement and the weight of the decoration you put on it. The mask can cover your face partially or totally. It can also be connected in the upper part with a head-dress or a crown. Suggested materials: light cardboard, leather, light wood.

When you choose to use cardboard, it is possible to glue on it a light rough canvas or other kinds of fabric which have a visible texture. If your mask resembles an animal or a nature spirit, then you can glue feathers, furs, leaves, or flowers on the entire surface of the mask. The mask needs to be fixed to your head by strings. Be sure to secure the strings firmly to the base of the mask: sometimes your dance can be very energetic!

The *decorations* are divided into two categories: colours, symbols, decorative patterns; and objects.

1 *Colours, symbols, decorative patterns.* You can give the mask a uniform colour and paint different symbols on it. If you like the texture and colour of the base of your mask, you can then simply paint symbols on it and later add objects. Remember that colours and symbols are powerful and create the personality of the mask. Suggested materials: gouache colours, designer colours, coloured clays, acrylic colours.

2 *Objects.* You can totally decorate your mask with them. Use elements from the animal, mineral and vegetable kingdoms: feathers, furs, bones, teeth, precious or semi-precious stones, flowers, leaves.

Provide yourself with scissors, knife-blade, glue and whatever other tools you choose.

Enjoy the magic of mask making!

Mandalas

Making mandalas is part of the Trance Dance Presenters' training. It empowers the presenters to create a sacred representation of their Trance Dance experiences.

Mandalas are designs symbolizing the universe. They allow the magical mind simply to flow, without the editing characteristics and the pretence of the conscious mind and ego. Mandalas reveal aspects of our personality which are normally beyond our awareness, allow greater understanding of our true selves, and provide us with information on how to heal ourselves. Mandalas are a sacred space within which we see a true reflection of our 'far memory' as revealed to us through Trance Dancing.

The materials you use will provide you with either less or greater flexibility. Mandalas can be made from almost any material: paint, marker pens, paper, leather, clay, stone, wood and any other material you choose to introduce.

The word mandala means 'centre' or 'magic circle'. The mandala reflects our total personality and lust to fulfil our potential in life at any given time. It is a central point, a source of energy; it is the way in which we express our true personality absent of our ego. The mandala also reflects our natural history, our innate connection to Mother Earth and all other living forms.

People who live close to nature express this point much more clearly. Black Elk, the Dakota Elder, said:

> Everything, the power of world, is done in a circle. The sky is round and I have heard the earth is round like a ball and so are all the stars; the wind in its greatest power whirls, birds make their nests in circles for theirs is the same religion as ours. The sun comes forth and goes down again in a circle. The moon does the same and both are round. Even the seasons form a great circle in their changing and always come back again to where they were. The life of a man is a circle from childhood to childhood and so it is in everything where power moves.

A divided circle was used by Etruscan soothsayers. The Egyptians and Persians saw the circle as sacred and the Celts used and worshipped the Silver Wheel of Arianrod as the place where blessed souls found their home. Stonehenge is a circular reflection of a celestial wheel to mark the progress of the circular sun through a circular year. Thousands of years of this form of worship resulted in the development of the Zodiac which is a wheel with 12 segments, also known as the Twelve Houses.

Many religious rituals and dances begin with the establishment of a sacred circle. Voodoo priestesses trace a circle on the ground as an invitation to the Gods. Native American shield makers begin their sacred work with a circle dance. Eskimos cut a circle in stone with repetitive rhythmic movements for a period of time in order to bring about a trance. Dervishes spin in the sacredness of the circle as a way to manifest celestial harmony. The dramatic end of the Sun Dance ceremony of the Plains Indians comes when the participants swing from ropes in a slow circle around a central pole.

The space within the ritual circle changes from an ordinary space to a sacred space. The circle is a reflection of the essence of life. Creating a circle is a sacred action. Creating a mandala is to create a sacred space which reflects that part of you which is sacred.

The mandala is also found in the Gothic cathedrals of Europe, in the rose-shaped and circular stained glass windows. The floor tile patterns of many early European churches and cathedrals were circular labyrinth mandalas. These floor mandalas represented the pilgrimage to the holy city of Jerusalem. Pilgrims would dance in celebration upon these labyrinths and mandalas.

The mandala gives us a map of our inner reality. It guides and supports the spiritual development of any of us who wish to advance to a state of higher consciousness and awareness.

Making a Mandala

The following are the seven steps in making mandalas.

1 It is important that you get into an altered state of consciousness, a trance, before you begin to draw. It may be helpful simply to relax, inhale deeply and, as you exhale, to imagine that tension, thoughts of the day, concerns, duties and obligations are all leaving your body. Clear your mind of all details until you find yourself in a deeply relaxed meditative state.

2 Once you are in trance, close your eyes if they are not yet closed and begin to focus your attention towards your centre. Begin to look inward. Notice feelings, forms,

colours and shapes that may be revealing themselves before the mind's eye. Using as little thought as possible, select a colour, form and feeling from your inner vision with your mind's eye as a starting point for your mandala. If nothing appears to you, simply go to the next step.

3 Open your eyes and look at the colours before you, guided by your inner feelings and vision, or simply respond to the colours as they present themselves to you. Choose a colour to begin your mandala with.

4 Draw a circle. Continue to use your thoughts as little as possible. Start filling in the circle with colour and form. You may start in the centre or around the edge of the circle. Work until you feel the mandala is completed.

5 Now identify the proper position of your mandala. To do this, turn it and look at it from all angles. Disregard the edges of the paper and look only at the design itself. Wait for your inner voice to say 'yes, this is the right position'. When you have found the proper position, mark the top of your mandala so that you are aware of how it should be placed or held.

6 Dating a mandala is helpful for future reference. Include the day, month and year. Knowing in which series certain forms and colours were drawn can help you to establish their meaning and more fully understand your personal evolution and communication with Spirit.

7 Place your mandala in front of you in the proper position and look at it. At this point imagine yourself very small and imagine that you are walking inside your mandala as if in a room or a landscape. Once inside your mandala, ask yourself how it feels to be there. Once you have experienced your feelings and thoughts within the mandala, give it a name. Write the name of your mandala at the bottom of the drawing.

Ritual Trance Dances

Ritual Trance Dance is the enactment of a culture's collective dream. It provides a way for the members of the society to interact with each other, gaining mutual and individual insights from Spirit.

The following are just a few ritual Trance Dances I use in trainings and in our shamanic retreats.

The Fire Dance

A huge fire thunders under the night sky; flames and sparks reach into the darkness of night. Around the dance ground, candles and incense fill the air. Suddenly naked humans appear from the body painting temple. As they dance around the fire their forms change from black silhouettes to brilliantly painted bodies.

The dancers then begin to chant, asking the fire Spirits to join in their dance. The ritual is being danced to drive out negative influences which then are pulled into the flames so they may emerge transformed into harmony and well-being.

Variation 1. Dancers may also carry unlit torches as they emerge from the temple of body painting. The torches should be handmade by them and consist of materials which actually represent things in their life they choose to transform: photos, clothing, eye glasses, jewellery, or any other symbol of the past. Dancers then crawl toward the fire to avoid the intense heat and put one end of the torch into the flames until it is ignited. Now they race around the fire showing their blazing torches in celebration as the flaming bits of their past disappear into sparks. Once the torch has burnt down and is too small to hold, they stop dancing, throw it in the fire, then sit and, as they watch it transform, acknowledge the value of their past.

Variation 2. Dancers actually wear clothing and accessories which represent their past, or a mask which conveys a personality they are willing to transform or to let go of. They dance about the fire in celebration and remove and throw into the flames any clothing and/or accessories which represent the past. The dancer may leave clothing on, or in fact be wearing other clothing underneath which represents their new self; some dancers may choose to strip to nakedness to symbolize their innocence and new beginning. To end this dance a gong is rung or a drum rolls and each dancer goes as close to the fire as they can, removes their mask and places it face up in the fire so they can witness the destruction or transformation of their old personality.

Ghost Killing Dance

The ghost to be killed in this dance may be alive or dead, may be an aspect of the dancer's personality that they wish to lose, or may be an actual person whom the dancer wants to remove from his or her life.

Each dancer must dress with symbols of weapons to be used to act out the ritual killing of the ghost.

1 The dancers, dressed, begin to dance around the fire; they yell, chant and mock the enemy, that person or that side of their personality – the shadow-side – which they wish to kill. They must really humiliate and ridicule the ghost to seduce it into showing itself. Unless the ghost is sufficiently provoked, it will not reveal itself.

2 Once the ghost manifests and its anger and rage has peaked, they go to the fire and take from it charcoal and begin to blacken their faces (black face paint may also be used) so their ego and personality disappear and they are invisible to the ghost they are going to kill. This is their advantage over the ghost. If they enter battle with

their ego or face showing, they will lose the battle for certain.

3 Then they dance out spontaneously a ritual battle and killing of the ghost using their symbols of weapons. Once the killing is complete, they must kneel around the fire acknowledging the value and profit of who or what they have killed.

In order for the ghost to stay dead and never return, the dancers must acknowledge the ghost's value in their life. To ensure this, they can also throw something of value which represents the deceased ghost into the fire.

Woman's Dance

1 All the women sit in a large circle around the fire, allowing enough space between them and the fire for the men to dance. They are dressed to seduce and attract men.

2 The women wear bandannas over their eyes. They begin to clap hands in rhythm together. They chant to the great Spirit descriptions of the men they want.

3 The men begin to dance around the fire, dressed to attract and seduce women. After the men have danced long enough to embody Spirit, they then choose the women they desire by dancing in front of them. The men are required to dance for at least three women.

4 The women remove their bandannas to watch the men trying to attract the women they desire.

5 As the men dance, the women laugh, yell to the men comments about their desires for them, and gossip with each other about the available men.

6 Then the men sit in a circle outside the women's circle and await the women who will now dance.

7 The women break their circle and begin to dance

seductively around the fire, each chanting the name of the man they are attracted to.

8   Then they break from the fire and each throws a blanket or cloth over herself and the man she desires, pulling him toward the fire. As they dance, the woman speaks to the man about what she wants from him. This is a great time to speak of sexual desires and ideas of marriage and childbirth, or to make up with past lovers.

9   The women have the say in choosing the man by taking him to dance with her under the shared blanket. Everyone should be dancing in pairs. When an odd number of dancers exists a group of three may be created if all are in agreement.

10 At some point, once the desires and intentions have been communicated, the women and their chosen men run off together. If the dancers want to have sex together, they observe their normal precautions. When there is more than one woman after the same man, the women must settle which one of them will get the man. This is done by bargaining, one woman giving gifts to the other woman in exchange for him or promising her some service. When a man wants a woman other than the one who has chosen him, he must give her a gift to her satisfaction in return for his release. This gift may be in the form of either goods or services.

Trance Dance and Drumming Circles

Spirit Moon events take place in participating TNI cities around the full and/or new moon of each month. It is a chance for us to reclaim our cultural birthright of 'Spirit rhythm consciousness' and for everyone to participate in the healing power of dance and percussion.

We at TNI have become part of a rhythmic reawakening

which will encourage a new generation to restore their birth-right and participate in the healing power of rhythm.

Rhythm produces certain fundamental results because of the natural laws of resonance and entrainment. Resonance is the natural ability of any substance such as wood, air, metal or living flesh to vibrate to a frequency from a source other than itself.

When we are surrounded by the powerful beat of drums and other percussion, the resonating systems of our body, bones, muscles, internal organs and nervous system including the brain, begin to vibrate in response.

Drumming alters brainwaves, entraining them from Beta which is the cycle of our daily activity and cognitive thought, into relaxed Alpha and eventually the trance state of Theta.

When we hear trance rhythms, all the parts of our brain come into activity. Our lower reptilian brain, our midbrain or mammalian brain, and our new brain or neo-cortex come into alignment and function as a unified whole.

Rhythm especially stimulates the 'alert system' of our reptilian brain. The loud repetitive drumbeat covers all other stimulus and sensory input, it blocks out the usual 'brain chatter' and causes the emotional and intuitive processes of the midbrain to come into the foreground. This induces trance, uncovers far memory and awakens non-linear creativity.

The healing alchemy of rhythm will transform any number of non-musicians into a foot stamping, hand smacking tribe, with ecstatic faces and eyes closing into trance. A communal beat emerges drawing participants into the time-less rhythm of the shaman.

Our ancestral societies used drumming to celebrate births, deaths, harvests, marriages, funerals and other rites of passage.

In tribal societies worldwide the drum has always been a reminder of our own heartbeat, our constant companion through the endless rhythms of life. Our life vibrates with rhythms as we quiver to our mother's pulse in her womb until our dying heart's final vibration at death. These and other rhythms in our life connect us to the timeless rhythms of day and night, new and full moon, seasons and stars.

For thousands of years humanity has expressed the pulse of life through rhythm. There has never been a society which has not expressed itself through the inner language of rhythm. From bone rattles to electronic drum machines, people have used percussion to synchronize themselves to the beat of the earth and the cosmos.

The pulse of the earth is hard to feel when we are running around in automobiles in a world covered in concrete. The beat of our heart is hard to hear when our ears are bombarded with the noise of traffic and the babble of television.

As we have lost touch with the Spirit of nature and the rhythms of our bodies and our planet we have also stopped creating a spiritual 'rhythm conscious' community. We have forgotten the pleasure and joyous healing of rhythmic rituals when people would play their drums and dance their dances together. These forgotten healing rhythms are further suppressed by a deeply ingrained belief, created by Christianity and other fundamental religions which link drumming and dancing to Satanic ritual.

All this will change as we create a wave of 'Spirit rhythm consciousness' through Trance Dance drumming circles. Our events are not oriented toward performance or musical skill but toward the transformation and expansion of human consciousness, the healing of our bodies, our planet and our community. Spirit Trance Dancing and drumming removes the isolation of the private beat of the Walkman and awakens us to our ancient shamanic rhythm, causing us to commune with nature.

As human beings have done for thousands of years we are

using percussion to bond with our friends and strangers, to express our joy and our anger and to transform and heal our pain.

Drumming and Trance Dancing spark our creativity, enlighten our physical and mental well-being, awaken our passionate Energizer, open our hearts and reveal the secret treasures of our Spirit intelligence.

When we dance and drum we are gently confronted with the risk of becoming part of something larger than us. We receive immediate feedback about our participation in our reality in that moment.

As we let go of inhibitions and allow Spirit to drum and dance through us our simple contribution joins an incomprehensible communal rhythm that not one of us can play alone. Then our separation disappears and we become part of something much bigger and more powerful than ourselves.

Race, gender and class become irrelevant as all melt together into an intimate and primal rhythm. The dance and the drums move us into that place beyond space and time where we all share the same magical beat, the same beat of our heart. Then time stops and we are together in now as one.

9 Trance Dance Experiences

Last night after the Trance Dancing I was watching the clouds hang down over Rio with Jesus standing there with his arms outstretched and the lights shooting up upon him and reflecting down off the clouds above him. It literally appeared as if Jesus was descending from the clouds, rather than standing on the cliff. This created the opportunity to test my ability to create my reality and I said, 'Let's see him dance.' Then he danced and I said, 'Okay, but his arms are always outstretched from this point of view. Let's see if you can make him turn around, so I don't see his arms.' And with that he began to float upward and make little short pulses or surges rather than dance movements, with a start, stop, start; and then he turned . . . he turned . . .

You find it hard to believe? But it's true. It happened. It happened to me and many similar reports have been given. We're talking about magic here, magic which occurs in an altered state of consciousness and is therefore not subject to physical law. *Understanding* is the murderer of magic and acceptance is essential to its presence. In this chapter, I'm going to let some others talk and describe to you what they have learnt and experienced on their travels to higher consciousness through the medium of Trance Dance.

My first experience of Trance Dance was in a group called 'Healing Ourselves' which was led by Frank in Paris. I was in a light trance and was swaying gently to the drumming music being played. My sense of the room and the people in it disappeared and I found myself surrounded by what I can only describe as Spirits in animal form. There were horses and eagles carrying me to a well that I recognized from this life. I then was greeted by a dark large cat which I knew to be a panther. The cat led me through the well and down through the earth in an incredibly long passage. At this point I started to feel the earth open and a pull to travel down into it. I became aware of my thoughts telling me that I was in Paris and in a group and that I had better be careful or I would disappear into the earth. I felt as though my whole body was going through the ground in two different realities. One of them was the seminar room in Paris and the other the well in the countryside. Somehow I knew that it was safe to carry on and I travelled down deeper into the earth. I experienced a beautiful sense of nature with many animal and other non-human life forms. At the end of the music Frank called us back into the room. I had not expected to experience this journey and had not been told that such a place existed. I kept my journey to myself at that time as I was unsure about sharing it with the group. The most incredible thing to me was that when I later found out about shamans, I learnt that they would take this journey regularly to the underworld to meet with their Spirit and power animals and also to retrieve soul parts for themselves and others. Frank teaches this way. He creates the opportunity for you to have the direct experience and after you have had the experience, he tells you where you can read about it. I had always regarded myself as cynical before this experience. I know now that my journey was as real as anything in my life and have since had an increasing respect for the Spirit world.

Alex, London, England

Trance Dancing is letting Spirit come inside you and move your body from within. Trance Dancing is a joyful act to celebrate life in its every form. It grounds you to the earth and it takes you to heaven; it's a wonderful way to heal yourself and others through fun and understanding, love and magic.

   As far as healing is concerned, I nourished my body, mind and Spirit through every dance, letting go of negative emotions and of negative thoughts by shaking them out, crying them out, laughing them out . . . as Spirit was coming in at each breath. I felt safe, being connected to the Source of all.

Khudai, Turin, Italy

It's magic and it's floating so gently and at the same time so intensely. And it's silence inside, a silence of abundance. So simple, breathing comes in and breathing goes out. Images, emotions, whole scenes appear and disappear and there is always me, coming towards and going away from myself, getting lost and coming back. Waves are coming in, waves of eternity. It was an experience in the mask-dance to see that I'm beautiful. Many times in my life I felt like hiding. Now I realize I'm hiding my beauty from others and myself. I always thought I was hiding my badness. This mis-understanding is clearing up.

Bhasha, Amsterdam, Holland

I have been a professional dancer for many years. I now do Trance Dance for myself at home as part of my training. I realize that I only learned here, now, how to dance, how to feel music. So gentle, deep and more real than any 'dance class' I ever had. I experienced total healing and transformation.

Zorah, Ibiza, Spain

During the Brazilian music I felt immediately very, very sad – as if I were Mother Earth. I felt a very deep connection to trees and plants. I felt as if I was Mother Earth and human beings were digging in my intestines. I felt in my body the rainforests and rivers that were being abused, especially in my heart and lungs. During this I felt huge anger, then I noticed that it was the anger of the people who were living in the rainforests. When I felt myself being Mother Earth I felt exhausted, at the end of my strength. Then I got angry again, because I thought of Mother Earth's fire inside, and I asked her why she does not kill her killers by using her huge force. Then she communicated that she will never do that and that her only connection to human beings is to nurture them. I realized that this will be my life's work: protecting Mother Earth and plants. This was the first time I felt at home on earth, she is my mother. This realization also enabled me to forgive my parents. I asked Mother Earth to give me her fire to help her, to give me energy for my heart.

Anna, Vienna, Austria

I cannot remember feeling this free in my entire 55 years of life. I experienced so many changes in my being. I am more clear in the way I look at things. I have lost almost all of my pre-judgement of things and people. I can now love without fear.

Healing has taken place physically. I have lived with a low blood sugar level for 30 years. I would become edgy, sweaty and have unclear thinking. Normally the only way to help this is to eat some protein or sugar in emergency. I suffered one of these 'attacks' during a break in the Trance Dance training. I had no time to eat. I returned to Trance Dancing. After five minutes of Trance Dancing my symptoms had completely disappeared, despite the fact that I ate nothing for another six hours. This has never happened to me before. I healed myself through the Trance Dance.

Douglas Achintya, Tübingen, Germany

The most magnificent gift I am receiving through Trance Dancing is the intimate friendship with my power animal. At the sound of the drumbeat Tiger leaps into me and his joy over being able to move, his passion and wildness are sometimes so overwhelming that I burst into tears.

As reward for letting him dance through me he slips into my dreams and journeys and teaches me to be a woman hunter. From him I learn to be invisible when it is wise. He teaches me how to gather all my power, all that I am, bring it all together, keep it, focus and hold it before the big, big leap. He is a sensual teacher, indulging in the pleasure and lust of our dance when the rhythms take possession of my body.

Sometimes during dancing a door opens and an answer is revealed to me about who I am and why I am here. During an American Indian Trance Dance I was shattered to the ground from sadness and desperation over the fate of my people, my loved ones, the family of my heart. All of them had been killed, abused and stamped upon. Around me I saw only death and pain; it was hopeless. The pain in my heart was so great it took every bit of my aliveness from me, I was unable to move and felt like dying. As the music changed rhythm, I felt some energy coming back into my body and I arose. More and more I felt uplifted and my aliveness returned: I danced a dance of power amongst the dead, I danced and made a vow. With every cell of my being I vowed for now and all times, to go beyond the sadness and become whole once again. I gave a vow to heal my heart, heal other hearts and our collective heart, in time to come.

Pamela, Miami, USA

My first experience with Trance Dance opened doors to inner space in a new way. Distant times and places suddenly became alive and explorable in a playful way that I had not experienced since childhood.

Since then I have Trance Danced the answers to questions

I did not even know I had. Going from being a separate point of consciousness, blending with the group of dancers, dancing into oneness – the energy that this creates has a tremendous healing power, reaching further than personal welfare. It is like a beautiful creation that in itself is bigger than the sum total of the parts.

Jeanne, Oslo, Norway

Ecstasy in Every Cell

One final testimony from Maruschi Adamah Magyarosy: she is a writer as well as a body and breath therapist and she attended the Trance Dance Presenters' training in Amsterdam in 1992. Here she describes her experience.

For months now a silent revolution has been swelling in my inner being, a revolution directed against everything that has anything to do with tradition, with dogmas, with pre-programmed exercises and with discipline. After 20 years of physical labour I have reached a point at which I know things cannot go on like this. I sense a deep aversion against telling those who take my courses and seminars exactly how to do a certain exercise, which they can then simply copy. I even catch myself despising them because they subject themselves to me mechanically, following my directions and believe they are doing something for themselves. At this turning point in my career I have met Frank Natale and he has touched a revolutionary vein in me that must have been dormant for a long time . . .

Frank gives us some final directions: the most important elements are rhythm, music, breathing, movement . . . the rest will take care of itself. I hear the first tones, start breathing and feel moved by the rhythm. Soon I feel like a living volcano which has been dormant for centuries and has waited for this particular moment to start spewing its flames in an endless, massive flow of lava. And the more I rave and spew, the more powerful the flow of energy and strength. Undefinable currents of aggression and anger, an inconceivable fury that may have existed for ages without my being aware of it, take possession of my elbows, thighs, knees and feet in strange movements. My head flies in all directions, as if it is trying to blow up my brain cells in order to drive out old established concepts and ideas from the darkest and remotest parts of my brains.

Trance Dance means turning the inner self inside out, letting yourself be guided by your soul, by your innermost powers. It is liberating, infinitely liberating . . .

The dance lasts for hours on end. Some 35 blindfolded participants are moving around me, each one of them occupied with his or her own process. Some enter the processes of fellow participants – singing, moving and jumping in musical and rhythmical harmony. I keep to myself and enjoy being in my own body as I never have before, not even during the most exciting sexual moments of my life.

This is you, says a voice from within me. This is your true self finally fighting to be allowed to reveal itself from inside. You are everything, you are able to dance in all roles without making any judgements. You are a man, you are a woman, you are an animal with all the qualities and abilities of that animal. You are a demon. I, your true self, know no boundaries. I know no values. Therefore I can reveal myself in all shapes and aspects, all colours, tones and clothing, from all cultures and all ages . . . You, your body, your intellect, your head – the only thing you need to do is to allow some free room for me, some space, time and freedom of movement . . . and, most important of all, an empty head, absent of old representations. Just love me inside you, acknowledge me in you and let me flow through you and take possession of you. The rest will take care of itself . . .

The voice never stops. It is a monologue within me – not, as usual, in my head but somewhere in my deep inner self, mercilessly and relentlessly confronting me with truths I have been unable, or unwilling, to see during all those years, simply because I was too much stuck on my usual everyday roles.

Trance Dance is mainly concerned with healing the 'trizophrenia' of the ego – that is, filling up the gap between thoughts, feelings and actions, recognizing thought impulses, in whatever form, and releasing them through movement. In this way it is possible to heal. According to Natale, the most important thing is to dance from the soul and not from the ego!

We all experience moments of absolute happiness: in our creativity, in nature, in love and in the few seconds of sexual climax. During those moments we are truly ourselves, authentic, goalless, wishless. Trance Dance allows you to extend those moments and to enjoy them time and again while still remaining completely free and absent of ideas. The thing is to let go, to recognize that what you believe is you in fact is unreal and to allow your greater reality to reveal itself through movement, breathing and rhythm . . .

Every move I make on the wooden floor feels like a call to Mother Earth, an ever-repeating mantra uttered effectively through the rhythmical movement of my naked feet. It is like knocking for entrance, asking her to take me back into her embrace. It is like a prayer for the healing of the earth, of the people and, of course, of myself. And suddenly I become Mother Earth, feel my belly grow larger and larger, turn into an ever-growing rhythmical, ecstatic woman's lap, swaying to the rhythms of the drum. I carry the cosmos in me, with all its treasures. But it is I, and I alone, who determines the origin – sex, form, race! Everything is born out of me, on all planes, whether they are children of the earth or the manifestation of my ideas and feelings. My body is a dancing universe in which all colours, forms and cultures exist.

Suddenly, despite my ecstasy, I become conscious of every single fibre in my body and of what I have read and taught so often: I am the creator of my own world, I am the eternal immortal Spirit who dances through its different forms beyond time and who engenders endless ecstasy in every single cell of my body and its many other bodies! And as the rhythm changes to become more violent, I again sense this overpowering force. Only this time the energy is of a purely masculine nature. It's as if I turn into a dancing light-penis which would like nothing better than to have sex with the entire universe. It grows, swelling beyond me and beyond itself. It fills me and the whole room with all the other dancers and starts to ejaculate in a shower of sparks. And suddenly I hear it again, that voice within me: I am the God of dance and do the dance of creation. I am eternal and immortal. Death is just a restricted, inflexible ego. Only your total surrender to me, the wish to dissolve into me and in your eternal Spirit, will enable you to be immortal and forever ecstatic. When all the knots in your brain and your heart are untied, the physical will become immortal even in this human life. This is the Lesson of all lessons!

This is it, the quintessence of experience with Frank Natale. Excited and completely exhausted I sink on the floor. A few moments later, bathed in tears and sweat, I hear a voice speaking as if from a wall of mist: Shiva is the god of destruction. But he is also the god of the dance who dances the dance of creation. Shiva as destructor means the annihilation, the dissolution of the ego. He breaks all chains, all handcuffs that prevent your transformation. He destroys and dissolves everything that has become superfluous . . . If you are willing to heal yourself, to heal your body and to heal the earth, the most important thing is to live completely in your body on the earth. Only then will you become whole, only then will you become immortal.

Conclusion

In conclusion I'd like to say that if we do not return home to our bodies, our nature and our planet we will continue to experience diseases we have no cure for, an environment against us rather than one which nurtures us. We will be a species so isolated from our spiritual and magical powers that we no longer trust and love, victims of male-dominated religion and science which cause us to deny our true identity – that of a multi-dimensional being who co-creates with the natural forces of the universe.

Trance Dancing and other shamanic practices close the distance between the physical world and our spiritual identity. We are much more than we have been told; we are immortal beings evolved over millions of years. We are very powerful and without a culture with a spiritual context we risk continuing the creation of negative, life-threatening results which cause us to feel like victims and desperately blame others for our hopeless situation.

My true aim is to bring to everyone's awareness spiritual practices such as Trance Dance, to resurrect shamanism in the West, its birth place, and to create a way of life which is spiritually sound and easy to access.

We are Westerners with a rich spiritual heritage which dates back 40,000 years. We must embrace our own roots and stop looking to Eastern mysticism or UFOs for answers to human problems.

It's time to take back our power, realize that being human is noble enough and continue to encourage ourselves and others to explore our potential.

I invite you to join us in this adventure by Trance Dancing and using the other tools for transformation we have provided.

Appendix 1

A NOTE FOR POTENTIAL AND ACTIVE TRANCE DANCE PRESENTERS

The TNI Trance Dance Presenters' training is an opportunity for you to work with a group of people who have already been involved in Trance Dance and therefore the energy and Spirit in the room is beyond verbal description. My experience is that the Spirit energy in the room is more intense than at any other Trance Dance events I have ever been to. It's an opportunity to dance to the exotic rhythms of Morocco, Egypt, aboriginal Australia, North American Indian cultures, India, Pakistan and the South Pacific, to name only a few; to share your experiences with a group of peers; to have your own direct contact with me. You also become part of a network of TNI Trance Dancers which means that you will receive a list of new music and, at times, copies of cassettes of new music.

When you have been cleared to be a TNI Trance Dance Presenter, you are responsible for all the dancers during your events. It is important that you understand the rule of non-interference, which is probably the most important rule of Trance Dancing, because the dancer's work is to respond to his or her own inner feelings and experiences. Any outside interference tends to interrupt this process and it is you as the Trance Dance Presenter who has to work at minimizing this kind of contact. This means avoiding making any un-necessary contact either verbally or non-verbally with the dancers while they are dancing, unless of course you are an experienced Trance Dance Presenter and have been ap-proved by me to interact with your dancers for the purposes of healing.

It is important as a Trance Dance Presenter to learn how to focus externally, to witness and observe your dancers, and even at times to act as a mirror to get a deeper understanding of the dancer's actions. You must also create a safe support-ive space for your dancers. It is fine for you to move to the rhythm yourself but it is even more important for you to focus externally on your dancers. If you start to respond too strongly to your own internal sensations, you are not staying outside and cannot focus enough to provide the necessary safety and support that your dancers need.

Situations may occur where you need to make light contact with the dancers in order to prevent them from crashing into another dancer, a wall or other physical objects. This contact should always be through touch, since the sound level of the music is usually too high for speech. Often when a dancer is in trance, words will immediately move them out of trance, while on the other hand light physical contact will not, especially when it is applied to non-threatening parts of the body such as the shoulders. When touching the shoulders or other non-threatening parts of the body, suggest the direc-tion of movement. This is best done when you are able to move the dancer within the rhythms which are being played.

To ensure the safety of all the dancers we recommend that you ask your dancers to remove wrist watches, sharp rings and other sharp jewellery. Obviously, your dancers are wearing bandannas and therefore glasses or lenses along with jewellery should be placed in a safe place before the dance begins.

Sometimes dancers fall and you need to accept this. They

may fall following violent movement or when spinning. It is generally impossible to avoid this and it usually occurs without damage. When such a fall seems imminent, allow it unless the head is in danger; even then, only cushion the fall rather than trying to stop it. Your primary responsibility is to protect the dancer's head from striking the floor, wall, or sharp object. Be clear that the fall is better than preventing the dancer from falling, in that the falling is an integral part of the dancer's inner experience. It is best to allow the person just to lie there for as long as they need to and allow them to get up in their own time rather than attempting to lift them back to their feet.

At times, dancers will come out of trance and fall to the floor in tears or anger. It is best to stay with the dancer from a distance, making no effort either to interrupt or enhance the crisis. The dancer may wish to return to the dance or to rest quietly. Either response is appropriate but be sure to let the dancer decide. Remember the rule of non-intervention. Be aware that this is their process, not yours, and very often it is a process of healing.

Sometimes dancers seem just to be standing or lying on the floor, and often it can be wrongly assumed that they are not in trance. Again, be clear that they are responding to their own inner process and this is just fine. They are not dancing to appease the expectations of yourself or anyone else. It is best to let people have their own dance and to refrain from judging or imposing your personal view upon it.

As the dance draws to a close, the music will start to fade. Be sure not to interfere with the dancers because very often they are dancing to the rhythm in the music, a rhythm which they continue to dance to after the actual music ends. Just let that happen.

Once your dancers have entered the integration phase, let them relax and be with the music. Be sure that the dance area is very quiet, peaceful and safe.

One of the better ways to end a session is in a circle. This circle is to give everyone a chance to complete their experience for themselves, to become grounded, and to return to their chosen space and time. Quite often during this period people have little to say since the dance experience is often very powerful and they may require some time to make sense of it, so do not force people to share, only provide the opportunity for them to do so.

I invite you to participate in our next Trance Dance Presenters' training so you may deepen your understanding of self and awaken your Energizer within.

Also, should you choose to, you will be empowered to present Trance Dance evenings and weekends as part of the TNI worldwide network of Presenters who are working to ensure the birth of a species of Trance Dancing Humans.

Appendix 2

THE NATALE INSTITUTE

The Natale Institute (TNI) is an international educational network, located in 11 countries, which offers seminars, trainings and retreats that have given thousands in the United States, Europe and Asia the ability to transform their thoughts into reality.

TNI was founded by Frank Natale, the spiritual elder of the Energizers and one of the world's leading contemporary healers. As TNI's director, Natale oversees a curriculum that effectively empowers the participants to reclaim their power as creators, healers, teachers and shamans.

TNI's material is directed toward:

1 Those who have made the choice to think shamanically
2 Those who intend to heal themselves and others
3 People who have power and are willing to manifest it
4 Those still busy reclaiming their power

TNI provides participants with the opportunity to become a teacher of all TNI material. TNI's participants achieve greater self-esteem, learn to communicate more effectively, learn to transform stress and anxiety into positive energy and to transform goals into concrete results. Through the use of workbooks, cassette tapes, rituals and channelled visualizations, the instructional material continues to manifest long after a seminar has been completed.

TNI brings into simple clear focus the enormously complex worlds of psychology, religion, shamanism, and plain old magic to be used for the purpose of clear direction and achievement.

We are about creating teachers who empower others to manifest, heal, create, laugh, love and live.

Appendix 3

COURSES, TAPES AND BOOKS

Courses

Natale conducts evening, weekend and week-long seminars, courses, trainings, rituals and retreats on a variety of topics throughout Europe, America and Asia. Shamans and instructors he has trained also teach TNI material.

Shamanism

Introduction To Shamanism: 'Journeying for Power'
Trance Dance Presenters' Training: 'The Dance of Life'
Soul Hunting Training: 'A Return to Spiritual Wholeness'
The Energizers' Training
Touch of Passion Training
Teacher Plant Training
Rites of Passage Training
Stolen Souls and Sexual Trauma Training
Shamanic Retreat (10 Days in Nature)

Life Skills

Manifesting Results: 'A Course in Creative Consciousness'
Effective Communication: 'The Experience of Being
  Understood'
Self-Esteem: 'The Power Within'
Mastering Alive Relationships: 'The 20 Qualities of Alive
  Relationships'
Honourable Sexuality: 'Acknowledging Our Origin'
The One Experience: 'Eight-Day Residential Intensive'

Tapes

Guided Visualizations

The visualizations listed below have been taken from TNI
seminars. Although they are extremely effective when used
outside the course context, we recommend that you participate in the seminar in order to experience their full power.
Other guidelines are as follows.

• Work with a whole set of five or seven visualizations,
  starting with number one and progressing to the last one.
  This will guarantee that you receive their full value.
• Work with each guided experience a minimum of three
  times before moving on to the next one. This will ensure
  total clarity and empowerment.
• Keep a diary and write down your experience after each
  visualization.
• Use other supportive techniques, such as writing affirma-
  tions from the visualizations and hanging them in visible
  locations, or using candles, pictures and other power
  symbols to remind you of the experience. This will
  enhance your growth.

Taped guided visualizations include the titles listed below. Tapes bought individually cost US $16.50/£11 each. See following list for series price.

'Embracing Our Higher Selves' (3 tapes at US $44.50/£29 for the set)
'The Lady of the Lake' (4 tapes at US $58.50/£39 for the set)
'The Power Within' (3 tapes at US $44.50/£29 for the set)
'Healing Ourselves' (3 tapes at US $44.50/£29 for the set)
'Channelling' (3 tapes at US $44.50/£29 for the set)
'Healing Your Eternal Friends' (3 tapes at US $44.50/£29 for the set).

Shamanism

These taped lectures are taken from the TNI Introduction evenings. The first two form the basis of the series and should be listened to first. Individual tapes cost US $16.50/£11. A set of 2 tapes costs US $28/£19.

'The Way of the Energizers' (Set of 2 tapes)
'Teacher Plant Hemp: The Miracle Power'
'Trance Dance: Dance of the Immortals'
'Soul Hunting: The Return of Spiritual Wholeness'

Bi-lateral Alignment ©

These tapes meditate you! They clear your brain, reduce stress and create an atmosphere that enhances creativity, self-hypnosis, relaxation etc. Each single tape costs US $16.50/£11. A set of 3 tapes costs US $44.50/£29 and a set of 6 costs US $83.50/£56.00. Titles available are:

'The Sea'
'Ambient OM'
'Mega OM'
'The Bamboo Flute'
'Mermaids of Atlantis'

Music (also available as CDs)

These cost US $15/£10 per cassette and US $21.50/£15 per CD.

'Trance Dance: The Breath of Fire'
'Trance Dance: Spirit Animal'
'Trance Dance: Shaman's Breath'
'Kissed by Lightning'
'Shamanic Journey'

Books

Mastering Alive Relationships (365 pages, US $26.50/£18)
Manifesting: A Course in Creative Consciousness (Portuguese language only, 173 pages, US $19/£13)

Further Information

Further information on seminars and courses can be obtained from your nearest main branch of The Natale Institute:

TNI France
M. Saiman
54 Chemin de Bellevue
78400 Chatou
France
Tel 33-1-30530348
Fax 33-1-30715506

TNI Germany
Schloss Str 90
12163 Berlin
Germany
Tel/Fax 49(0)-30-7973555

TNI Italy
K. Apurva Mastinu
Via Superga 32/1-10020
Baldissero T sc
Torino
Italy
Tel/Fax 39-11-836561

The Natale Institute
The Crystal Palace
Haarlemmerstraat 116
1013 EX Amsterdam
The Netherlands
Tel 31(0)20-623 3781
Fax 31(0)20-638 4969

TNI USA
PO Box 163594
Austin, TX 78716
USA
Tel 1-512-708-8888
Fax 1-512-708-8118

Books, tapes and CDs can be obtained from:

*Tools for Transformation
International*
Via Gaia 72
36100 Vicenza
Italy
Tel/Fax 39(0)444-300 398

All the prices given here for tapes, CDs and books include postage and handling. Please enclose a cheque with your order.

Useful Addresses

TRANCE DANCE PRESENTERS

Australia

Shazar Robinson
159 Belmore Rd
NSW 2031 Randwick
Australia

Austria

Katherina Suravi Schmid
Hetzendorfstr 97/3/9
1120 Vienna
Tel 43 1-8024700

Girike Linser
Am Stadtberg 1
6330 Kufstein
Tel 43-537262296

Brazil

Rohit Mahon
Rue Arcipreste Manoel
   Teodoro 245
Casa 85
66023-690 PA Belem
Tel/Fax 55-91-222 3614

Finland

Anna Tosha Einioe
TNI Finland
Ramsaynranta 1 A1
00330 Helsinki
Finland
Tel 358(0)0-486 301

France

Anna Eyraud
49 Rue de Charonne
75011 Paris
Tel 33-1-48 07 1837

Irène Michael
61 G. rue Jules Ferry
78400 Chatou
Tel 33-1-30 71 17 61

Aude Prior
Centre Au-Delà
Aviernoz
74570 Thorens/Glières
Tel 33-50 22 49 25

Sandra Rouyer
171 Rue de Fg.
  Poissonnière
75009 Paris
Tel 33-1-45 26 99 72

Margaret Saiman
TNI Ouvertures
54 Chemin de
  Bellevue
78400 Chatou
Tel 33-1-30 53 03 48
Fax 33-1-30 71 55 06

Divine Saiman
18 Rue Cardinet
75017 Paris
Tel 33-1-42 12 05 48

Germany

Antonella Bianco
Schloss Str 90
12163 Berlin
Tel/Fax 49(0)-30-7973555

Marlene Bornhütter
Alfons Lindemann
Nusshecke 1
35444 Bieberthal
Tel 49(0)6409-1246

Madak Angela Fiege
Mendelssohnstr 78
22761 Hamburg
Tel 49(0)40-890 2247

Vidhy Liebau
Zum Bergwerk 12
60437 Frankfurt
Tel 49(0)69-501 688

Kathrin Pohl
Im Holzmoor 23
38108 Braunschweig
Tel 49(0)531-374 629

Achintya and Neerja
  Schröder-Platz
Brühlhof 10
72072 Tübingen
Tel 49(0)7472-6249

Signe Schuhmacher
Lange Str 57
17489 Greifswald
Tel 49(0)3834-2516

Divyam Visser
Bavariastr 21
80336 Munich
Tel 49(0)89-725 4434

Italy

TNI Italy
K Apurva Mastinu
Via Superga 32/1-10020
Baldissero T.sc.
Torino
Tel 39-(0)11-940 7485

TNI Friendship
Shaida Cartella
Buddhaprem Enria
Via Balbo 6
10124 Torino
Tel/Fax 39(0)11-836 561

TNI Vicenza
Loredana Garbuio
Andrea Refosco
Via G. Galilei 1
36057 Arcognano VI
Tel 39(0)444-300 398

TNI Varese
Khalis Mattoni
Nandra Carolo
Via Astico 40
21100 Varese
Tel 39(0)332-229 146

TNI Bergamo
Via Grumello 61
24100 Bergamo
Tel 39(0)35-403 284

TNI Milano
Giuseppe Lotito
Via Gratosoglio 46
20142 Milano
Tel 39(0)2-893 010 24

TNI Bari
Regina Gambatesa
Piazza Moro 55
70100 Bari
Tel 39(0)80-5210908

M. Cloude Eberlyn
Via Belfore 38
10125 Torino
Tel 39(0)11-655 879

Silvia Bondi
Katya Haudemand
C.so Vigevano 49
10100 Torino
Tel 39(0)11-859 626

The Netherlands

Brigitte Allhenn
Voorthuizenstr 49
1106 DJ Amsterdam
Tel 31(0)20-696 5027

Joy Andela
Grotestraat 65
6511 VB Nijmegen
Tel 31(0)80-223 334

Jason Natale
Haarlemmerstr 116
1013 EX Amsterdam
Tel 31(0)20-623 3781
Fax 31(0)20-638 4969

Norway

Jeanne Kampel and
   Eline Huitfeldt
Hoybovn 12c
Malmoya
0198 Oslo 1
Tel 47(0)2-287 095

Shantam Kielland
Prinsessealleen 15
0275 Oslo 2
Tel 47-(0)2-556828

Spain

Zorah Fischer
Disco Gallery
Calle Carlos V 12
7820 Ibiza
Tel 34(0)71-310 374
Fax 34(0)71-317 064

Lourdes Guerrero
Apdo 1125
Ibiza
Fax 34(0)71-312 770

Switzerland

Salila Wenzl
Waldhaus Zentrum
Kanalweg 1
CH-3432 Lützelflüh
Tel 41-(0)34-610 705
Fax 41-(0)34-616 550

United Kingdom

Alexis Brown
TNI London
22 Wordsworth Walk
London NW11 6AU
Tel 44(0)181-458 8638
Fax 44(0)171-625 5203

Cynthia Harris
12 Harvey Road
London N8 9PA
Tel 44(0) 181-341-5000

Sarah Warwick
47 Ladbroke Square
London W11 3ND

USA

Wilbert Alix or
   Heather McKissick
TNI Texas
PO Box 163594
Austin, TX 78716
Tel 1-512-708 8888
Fax 1-512-708 8118

Hala Ayla
214 Panoramic H'way
Mill Valley, CA 94941
Tel/Fax 1-415-383-8970

Missy Carricarte
6090 SW 40th Street
Miami, FL 33155
Tel 1-305-858-9495

Ralph Cissne
409 Pacific Coast H'way, No
   465
Redondo Beach, CA 90277
Tel 1-310-372-1585
Fax 1-310-372-5186

David Cusak
4150 Latigo Canyon Road
Malibu, CA 90265
Tel 1-310-589 5737

Russel Haack
1895 Alpine Ave, No 16D
Boulder, CO 80304
Tel 1-303-449-6009

Eric L. Martinsen
411 Brook Street #1
Clinton, MA 01510
Tel 1-508-368 8766

Fonda Shannon
8523 Stagewood Drive
77338 Humble, TX
Tel 1-713-446-6351

Kat Robin Sun
261 Forrest Glen Circle
Atlanta, Georgia
Tel 1-404-508-8743

Cynthia Zieto
6541 Red Deer Str
San Diego, CA 92122
Tel 1-619-558 8047